# Sensational Centers

## Table of Contents

D0719953

# Table of Contents

# Table of Contents

# About This Book

Your friends at *The Mailbox*® have done it again! *Sensational Centers* is a terrific collection of over 200 skilled-based, creative learning centers you can use to supplement your curriculum. Select from a variety of motivating activities to reinforce essential skills in core curriculum areas—literacy, math, and science as well as special holidays and seasons—and meet your students' individual needs.

For each center we provide step-by-step instructions, including a detailed materials list, and simple directions for setting up and using the center. Tailoring skills practice has never been easier for you to implement or more fun for your students!

## Suggestions for Setting Up and Using Learning Centers

- Determine a designated center work area and how many centers you will feature.
- Organize your materials to allow students easy access and cleanup.
- Determine a center schedule: Have students work independently during the week, include the centers as part of your group-work schedule, set aside daily or weekly center time, or use the centers as a teaching aid when working with a small group of students.
- Show students how to complete the centers and check their answers, if appropriate.
- Create a designated area for students to place their completed work and a display area for students' creations.
- Determine how you will evaluate and track students' progress.
- Be sure to share students' center success with their family members!

**Project Editor:** Elizabeth H. Lindsay
**Staff Editors:** Denine T. Carter, Sherri Lynn Kuntz, Scott Lyons, Leanne Stratton, Deborah G. Swider, Hope H. Taylor
**Contributing Writers:** Nancy Anderson, Cindy Barber, Amy Barsanti, Eleanor Beson, Beverly Bippes, Rebecca Brudwick, Lisa Bucholz, Danielle Conforti, Candi Deal, Kathleen DiGrigoli, Heather Graley, Polly B. Hoffman, Cynthia Holcomb, Linda Masternak Justice, Betsy Liebmann, Linda Macke, Leslee McWhirter, Geoffrey Mihalenko, Laura Mihalenko, Carol Ann Perks, Jennifer Overend Prior, Katie Robinson, Debbie Rovin-Murphy, Leann Schwartz, Becky Shelley, Valerie Wood Smith, Darcy Soule, Ann Marie Stephens, Laura Wagner
**Copy Editors:** Gina Farago, Karen Brewer Grossman, Karen L. Huffman, Amy Kirtley-Hill, Debbie Shoffner
**Cover Artists:** Clevell Harris, Nick Greenwood, Kimberly Richard
**Art Coordinator:** Clevell Harris
**Artists:** Pam Crane, Teresa R. Davidson, Nolan Galloway, Theresa Lewis Goode, Clevell Harris, Sheila Krill, Mary Lester, Clint Moore, Kimberly Richard, Greg D. Rieves, Rebecca Saunders, Barry Slate, Donna K. Teal
**Typesetters:** Lynette Maxwell, Mark Rainey

**President, The Mailbox Book Company**™: Joseph C. Bucci
**Director of Book Planning & Development:** Chris Poindexter
**Book Development Managers:** Stephen Levy, Elizabeth H. Lindsay, Thad McLaurin, Susan Walker
**Curriculum Director:** Karen P. Shelton
**Traffic Manager:** Lisa K. Pitts
**Librarian:** Dorothy C. McKinney
**Editorial and Freelance Management:** Karen A. Brudnak
**Editorial Training:** Irving P. Crump
**Editorial Assistants:** Terrie Head, Melissa B. Montanez, Hope Rodgers, Jan E. Witcher

## www.themailbox.com

# Literacy

# Alphabet Stew

**Skill:** Alphabetizing

**Materials needed:**
- an assortment of plastic vegetables
- a permanent marker
- a large cooking pot
- a ladle
- a large paper plate
- a class supply of paper
- pencils

**Setting up the center:**
1. Use the permanent marker to program each plastic vegetable with a desired word.
2. Place the vegetables in the cooking pot.
3. Display the cooking pot, ladle, paper plate, paper, and pencils at a center.

**Using the center:**
1. A student scoops two ladles full of vegetables onto her plate. (If the ladle is small, the student may need additional scoops of vegetables.)
2. She arranges the programmed words in alphabetical order on her plate and then copies them onto a sheet of paper.
3. If time allows, she may serve herself another helping of stew.

# Animal Crackers

**Skill:** Alphabetizing

**Materials needed:**
- a shoebox with a lid
- markers
- a variety of animal-shaped cutouts

**Setting up the center:**
1. Decorate the shoebox to resemble a box of animal crackers.
2. Label each cutout with the name of the animal.
3. Arrange the cutouts in alphabetical order and then number the back of each one in sequential order.
4. Place the cutouts in the decorated shoebox and display the box at a center.

**Using the center:**
1. A student removes the cutouts from the box.
2. He arranges the words in alphabetical order.
3. The student turns over the cutouts to check his work.

# Shopping With "Alpha-Betty"

**Skill:** Alphabetizing

**Materials needed:**
- a supply of toy catalogs
- a supply of 4" x 6" notecards
- glue
- markers
- a class supply of the shopping list form on page 36
- a small basket
- pencils

**Setting up the center:**
1. Cut out and glue pictures from toy catalogs onto the notecards (one picture to a card).
2. Program each notecard with the item's name.
3. Display the notecards, basket, forms, and pencils at a center.

**Using the center:**
1. A student selects five cards from the basket and arranges the programmed words in alphabetical order.
2. She copies the items onto her shopping list.
3. She returns the cards to the basket.
4. The student repeats the activity until she has made a total of four shopping lists.

# Spaghetti Spelling

**Skill:** Spelling

**Materials needed:**
- a copy of a current spelling list
- a clean, empty spaghetti sauce jar
- a supply of white yarn, cut into pieces of varying lengths
- a large cooking pot
- a placemat

**Setting up the center:**
1. Cut the spelling list apart so that each word is on a separate strip of paper.
2. Place the strips of paper in the jar.
3. Place the yarn pieces in the cooking pot.
4. Display the jar, pot, and placemat at a center.

**Using the center:**
1. A student removes a word strip from the jar.
2. He takes one (or more) length of yarn from the pot, puts it on the placemat, and uses it to form a letter of the word.
3. He continues taking lengths of yarn from the pot to spell the entire word.
4. The student returns the yarn to the pot and, if time allows, selects another word to spell.

# All in a Row

**Skill:** Identifying rhyming words

## Materials needed:
- 20 craft sticks
- a permanent marker
- a list of rhyming word pairs
- a jar or similar container

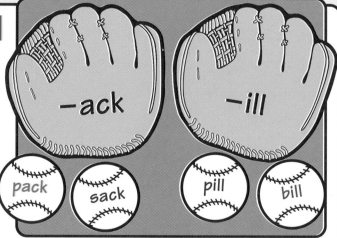

## Setting up the center:
1. Use the marker to divide each craft stick in half as shown.
2. Label the sticks so that one word of each rhyming pair is written on a different stick.
3. Place the sticks in the container and display the container at a center.

## Using the center:
1. A student pair begins the activity by placing one stick from the container onto the table or workspace.
2. Each partner then takes five sticks from the container.
3. The first player tries to match a rhyming word from her supply to a stick on the table. If she makes a match, she lays her stick down with the rhyming words side by side and her turn is over. If a child can't make a match, play continues with the other player.
4. The first student to use all the sticks from her supply is the winner.
5. If time allows, the pair places the gathered sticks back in the container and plays another round.

# Catch a Rhyming Word

**Skill:** Recognizing word families

## Materials needed:
- a supply of brown construction paper cutouts of the mitt pattern on page 37
- a supply of white construction paper cutouts of the baseball pattern on page 37
- markers
- a baseball cap

## Setting up the center:
1. Program each mitt with a different rime such as –ack, –ice, –ill, or –uck.
2. For each rime, program a set of baseballs. Label each ball in the set with a word that ends with the chosen rime.
3. On the back of each mitt, list the words that belong in the rime group.
4. Place the mitts and balls in a baseball cap. Display the cap at a center.

## Using the center:
1. A student removes the mitts from the baseball cap and arranges them on the table or workspace.
2. He reads the word on each baseball and places it on the mitt with the matching rime.
3. After placing all the baseballs, he turns over each mitt to check his work.

# Lots of Legs

**Skill:** Discriminating vowels

**Materials needed:**
- 1 construction paper cutout of the caterpillar pattern on page 38
- 10 construction paper cutouts of the foot patterns on page 38
- markers
- a large resealable plastic bag

**Setting up the center:**
1. Program each segment of the caterpillar's body with a different long-vowel sound.
2. For each long vowel, program two feet, each with a different word containing that vowel sound.
3. Label the back of the caterpillar with the correct words for self-checking.
4. Store the pieces in the resealable bag. Display the bag at a center.

**Using the center:**
1. A student removes the caterpillar and feet from the bag.
2. She reads the word on each foot and places it under the matching segment of the caterpillar.
3. After placing all the feet, she turns over the caterpillar to check her work.

# Chilly / Vowel Sounds

**Skill:** Discriminating vowels

**Materials needed:**
- a construction paper gameboard, decorated as shown
- a supply of construction paper ice cubes
- markers
- a resealable plastic bag

**Setting up the center:**
1. Program each ice cube with a word containing a long *i* or a short *i* vowel sound.
2. Write the corresponding vowel symbol on the back of each cube.
3. Laminate the gameboard and ice cubes for durability, if desired.
4. Store the ice cubes in the resealable bag.
5. Display the gameboard and bag of ice cubes at a center.

**Using the center:**
1. A student removes the ice cubes from the bag and reads each word.
2. If the word has a short *i* sound, he places the ice cube on the igloo. If the word has a long *i* sound, he places the ice cube on the icebox.
3. After placing all the ice cubes, the student turns them over to check his work.

# Short *U* Pup

**Skill:** Discriminating vowels

**Materials needed:**
- a construction paper gameboard, decorated as shown
- a supply of construction paper bones
- markers
- a resealable plastic bag

**Setting up the center:**
1. Program each bone with a word containing a long *u* or a short *u* vowel sound.
2. Write the corresponding vowel symbol on the back of each bone.
3. Laminate the gameboard and bones for durability, if desired.
4. Store the bones in the resealable bag.
5. Display the gameboard and bag at a center.

**Using the center:**
1. A student removes the bones from the bag and reads each word.
2. If the word has a short *u* sound, she places it by the pup. If the word has a long *u* sound, she places it on the doghouse.
3. After placing all the bones, the student turns them over to check her work.

# Syllable Softball

**Skill:** Counting syllables

**Materials needed:**
- 3 brown construction paper cutouts of the mitt pattern on page 37
- markers
- a 12" x 18" sheet of colorful construction paper
- glue
- a supply of white construction paper cutouts of the softball pattern on page 37
- a resealable plastic bag

**Setting up the center:**
1. Program each mitt with the number 1, 2, or 3. Glue the mitts to the construction paper.
2. Program each softball pattern with a one-, two-, or three-syllable word. Label the back of each ball with the correct number of syllables in the word.
3. Store the softballs in the resealable bag. Display the mitt poster and bag at a center.

**Using the center:**
1. A student removes the softballs from the bag. He reads each word and determines how many syllables it contains.
2. He places each softball on top of the mitt with the matching number of syllables.
3. After placing all the softballs, the student turns them over to check his work.

# Flower Power

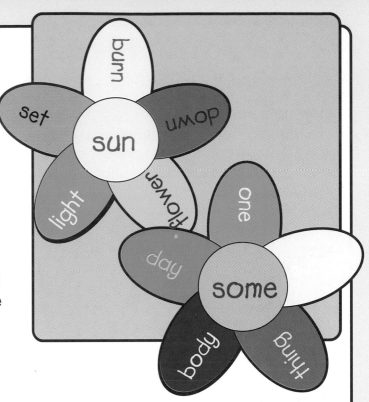

**Skill:** Making compound words

**Materials needed:**
- three 2" construction paper circles
- fifteen 3"-long construction paper petals
- fine-tipped markers
- a large resealable plastic bag

**Setting up the center:**
1. Program each circle and petal as shown.
2. Program the back of each circle with a list of the resulting compound words. Laminate the circles and petals for durability, if desired.
3. Store the pieces in the resealable bag and display it at a center.

**Using the center:**
1. A student removes the construction paper pieces from the bag.
2. She places the circles so that the compound word parts are faceup.
3. She selects a petal, placing it near a circle to form a compound word.
4. After placing all the petals, she turns over the circles to check her work.

# Compound Pairs

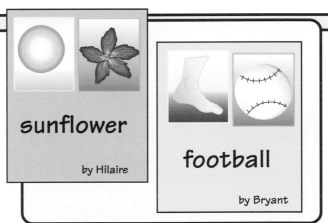

sunflower
by Hilaire

football
by Bryant

**Skill:** Making compound words

**Materials needed:**
- a supply of magazines
- a supply of light-colored construction paper
- scissors
- glue
- markers

**Setting up the center:**
1. Create a center sample by finding and cutting out from a magazine two pictures of objects whose names can be used to make a compound word. Glue the pictures to a sheet of construction paper, labeling the paper with the resulting compound word. (See the examples shown.)
2. Display the sample and the materials at a center.

**Using the center:**
1. A student finds and cuts out from a magazine two pictures of objects whose names can be used to create a compound word.
2. He glues the pictures to a sheet of construction paper, labeling the paper with the resulting compound word.
3. He continues the activity, making a predetermined number of compound words.
4. If desired, collect the completed student pages and bind them together into a class book of compound words.

# Root Garden

**Skill:** Identifying base words

**Materials needed:**
- a supply of small flowerpots
- a supply of construction paper flowers
- a supply of craft sticks
- a permanent marker
- glue
- an 8½" x 11" white envelope

**Setting up the center:**
1. Program each flowerpot with a different base word.
2. Program each flower with a word derived from one of the base words.
3. Glue each flower to a craft stick.
4. Decorate the front of the envelope to resemble a seed package. Label the back of the envelope with an answer key.
5. Display the flowerpots, flowers, and envelope at a center.

**Using the center:**
1. A student selects a flower and reads its programmed word.
2. She determines its base word and places it in the corresponding pot.
3. After placing all the flowers, she checks her work using the answer key.

# Poppin' Plurals

**Skill:** Adding -s or -es

**Materials needed:**
- 2 popcorn tubs
- a supply of yellow self-adhesive dots
- a supply of cotton balls
- a fine-tipped marker
- a resealable plastic bag

**Setting up the center:**
1. Label one popcorn tub with the suffix -s and the other tub with -es.
2. Program half the yellow dots with nouns to which -s can be added. Program the remaining half with nouns to which -es can be added.
3. Stick each dot to a cotton ball.
4. Label the bottom of each popcorn tub with the correct nouns for self-checking.
5. Store the cotton balls in the resealable bag. Display the popcorn tubs and bag at a center.

**Using the center:**
1. A student removes the cotton balls from the bag.
2. He reads the word on each cotton ball and places it in the matching tub.
3. After placing all the cotton balls, he empties each container and turns over the tubs to check his work.

# Soaring Synonyms

**Skill:** Identifying synonyms

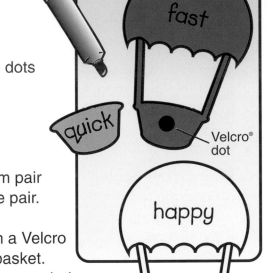

**Materials needed:**
- construction paper cutouts of the balloon and basket patterns on page 39
- markers
- Velcro® self-adhesive dots
- a sheet of paper
- a manila envelope

**Setting up the center:**
1. Program each balloon cutout with one word of a synonym pair and each basket cutout with the remaining word from the pair.
2. Create an answer key on the separate sheet of paper.
3. Laminate the pieces for durability, if desired. Then attach a Velcro dot to the bottom of each balloon and the back of each basket.
4. Staple the balloons to a bulletin board where students can reach them.
5. Store the baskets and answer key in the manila envelope. Display the envelope near the bulletin board center.

**Using the center:**
1. A student selects a basket from the envelope and determines which balloon has its matching synonym.
2. She attaches the basket to its corresponding balloon using the Velcro dots.
3. After all the baskets have been placed, she uses the answer key to check her work.

# Grade-A Antonyms

**Skill:** Identifying antonyms

**Materials needed:**
- 36 self-adhesive dots
- an empty egg carton
- 12 plastic eggs
- a permanent fine-tipped marker
- a basket

**Setting up the center:**
1. Program 12 adhesive dots, each with one word of an antonym pair.
2. Place each programmed dot in a different section of the egg carton.
3. Program each plastic egg with the remaining word from an antonym pair.
4. For self-checking, program a second set of dots to match those in Step 1. Take each egg apart and attach its antonym answer sticker on the inside.
5. Place all the eggs in the basket.
6. Display the egg carton and basket at a center.

**Using the center:**
1. A student chooses an egg from the basket and reads its programmed word.
2. He places the egg in the carton atop its matching antonym.
3. After placing all the eggs, he opens each egg to check his work.

# Opposites Attract

**Skill:** Identifying antonyms

**Materials needed:**
- ¹/₂ sheet of poster board, decorated as shown
- a supply of self-adhesive magnetic tape
- a supply of tagboard squares (including 1 larger square)
- markers
- a resealable plastic bag

**Setting up the center:**
1. Program the poster with one word each from a number of antonym pairs.
2. Place a strip of magnetic tape above each word.
3. Write each remaining word from the antonym pairs on a separate square of tagboard. Attach a strip of magnetic tape to the back of each tagboard square.
4. Create an answer key on the separate, larger square of tagboard.
5. Store the squares and answer key in the resealable bag. Display the poster and bag at a center.

**Using the center:**
1. A student removes the tagboard squares from the bag.
2. She reads each word and places it on the magnetic strip above its matching antonym on the poster.
3. After placing all the squares, the student checks her work using the answer key.

# Word Soup

**Skill:** Word building

**Materials needed:**
- a supply of plastic letters
- a large bowl
- a class supply of lined paper
- pencils

**Setting up the center:**
1. Place the plastic letters in the bowl.
2. Display the bowl, paper, and pencils at a center.

**Using the center:**
1. A student takes six letters from the bowl.
2. He writes the letters at the top of a sheet of paper.
3. He arranges one or more of the plastic letters to spell a word.
4. Each time a word is made, he writes it on his paper.
5. If time allows, he may take another set of six letters and repeat the activity.

# On Track With Contractions

**Skill:** Identifying contractions

**Materials needed:**
- a supply of construction paper cutouts of the train and track patterns on page 40
- a marker
- a manila envelope

**Setting up the center:**
1. Program each train track with a contraction.
2. On the back of each train track, write the two words used to form the contraction.
3. Program one word of the contraction on an engine and the other word on a train car.
4. Store the cutouts in a manila envelope. Display the envelope at a center.

**Using the center:**
1. A student removes the train and track cutouts from the envelope and separates them by shape.
2. She reads the contraction on a train track and finds the matching words on an engine and a car.
3. After placing all the train cutouts on the tracks, she turns over the tracks to check her work.

# Possessive or Contraction?

**Skill:** Identifying words with apostrophes

**Materials needed:**
- a selection of books
- a class supply of the "Possessive or Contraction?" form on page 41
- pencils

**Setting up the center:**
  Display the materials at a center.

**Using the center:**
1. A student selects a book and finds a word with an apostrophe.
2. He records the word on the form, determines if it is a possessive or a contraction, and then writes the meaning of the word. (For example, *she's* can mean *she is,* and *Bob's* can mean *belonging to Bob.*)
3. He continues the activity until his chart is complete.

Name _Daryl_

**Possessive or Contraction?**

Identifying words with apostrophes

| Word Found | Possessive or Contraction? | What It Means |
|---|---|---|
| David's | possessive | belonging to David |
| isn't | contraction | is not |
| shouldn't | contraction | should not |
| cat's | possessive | belonging to the cat |
| that's | contraction | that is |
| what's | contraction | what is |
|  | possessive |  |

# Dictionary Detectives

**Skill:** Using a dictionary

**Materials needed:**
- 3 small containers
- twenty 2" squares of green, gray, and blue tagboard
- a permanent marker
- a dictionary
- a class supply of paper
- pencils

**Setting up the center:**
1. Program the green and blue squares with the numbers 1–20.
2. Program half the gray squares with the letter *A* and the remaining half with the letter *B*.
3. Store the green squares in the first container and label it "Pages." Store the gray squares in the second container and label it "Columns." Store the blue squares in the third container and label it "Words."
4. Display the containers, dictionary, paper, and pencils at a center.

**Using the center:**
1. A student takes a card from each container.
2. She opens the dictionary to the page specified on the green card. She looks to find the column specified on the gray card. She then counts down the number of words designated by the blue card.
3. The student writes the word on her paper, returns the cards to the containers, and repeats the activity a predetermined number of times.

# "Thesaur-o-saurus"

**Skill:** Using a thesaurus

**Materials needed:**
- a class supply of the dinosaur form on page 42
- a marker
- a thesaurus
- pencils

**Setting up the center:**
1. Program each dinosaur with a word found in the thesaurus.
2. Display the forms, thesaurus, and pencils at a center.

**Using the center:**
1. A student takes one programmed dinosaur form and reads the word.
2. He locates the word in the thesaurus.
3. He finds five synonyms for the word, writing each word on one of the dinosaur's spikes.
4. The student turns his form over and writes a sentence for each synonym he listed.

# Poem Puzzles

**Skill:** Sequencing

**Materials needed:**
- a short poem with which your students are familiar
- scissors
- a class supply of resealable plastic bags
- glue
- a class supply of white construction paper
- crayons or markers

**Setting up the center:**
1. Type a copy of the poem in large print and duplicate to make a class set, plus one extra.
2. Cut apart the lines of each poem in the class set and store the pieces for each complete set in a separate resealable bag.
3. Display the bags, glue, construction paper, crayons or markers, and a complete copy of the poem at a center.

**Using the center:**
1. A student removes the poem pieces from a bag.
2. She reads the pieces and then arranges the pieces, or lines of the poem, in the correct order.
3. She glues the sequenced poem to a sheet of construction paper.
4. She illustrates her completed poem.

# HATS OFF TO COLORS!

**Skill:** Reading color words

**Materials needed:**
- a supply of 8" construction paper circles, one to match each color word
- scissors
- glue
- a stapler
- a supply of index cards
- markers
- a supply of colored curling ribbon to match the construction paper colors

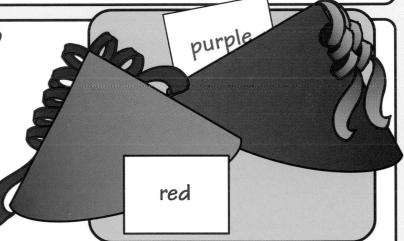

**Setting up the center:**
1. Cut a slit from the edge to the center of each construction paper circle.
2. Overlap and then glue the resulting edges to make cone-shaped hats.
3. Staple matching curling ribbon to the top of each hat.
4. Program each index card with a color word corresponding to each hat.
5. Write the corresponding color word inside each hat.
6. Display the hats and index cards at a center.

**Using the center:**
1. A student matches each color word to the corresponding colored hat.
2. He lifts the hats to check his answers.

# Read the Room

**Skill:** Recognizing words

**Materials needed:**
- 2 holiday or seasonal cutouts
- tape
- dowel-type pointer stick

**Setting up the center:**
1. Tape the seasonal cutouts back-to-back. Tape the resulting double-sided cutout over one end of the pointer as shown.
2. Display the pointer at a center.

**Using the center:**
1. In turn, each student in a pair uses the pointer to identify five words posted around the classroom. The student reads aloud each word as she points to it.
2. Student pairs continue pointing to words and reading them for a predetermined time or number of turns.

# Fido's Facts and Opinions

**Skill:** Determining fact and opinion

**Materials needed:**
- a brown paper gift bag
- markers
- a supply of bone-shaped construction paper cutouts, one larger than the others

**Setting up the center:**
1. On the front of the gift bag, draw a doghouse similar to the one shown.
2. Label one side of the resulting doghouse "Facts" and the other side "Opinions."
3. Program a set of bone-shaped cutouts each with a different number and fact or opinion statement. Program the larger bone with an answer key.
4. Store the bones inside the decorated bag and display the bag at a center.

**Using the center:**
1. A student removes the bones from the bag.
2. He reads each statement and then places it by the appropriate side of the doghouse.
3. After all of the bones have been placed, he uses the answer key to check his work.
4. For an added challenge, place a supply of blank bones at the center. Have each student write "fact" or "opinion" on one side of a cutout and a matching statement on the other side. Display student statements at the center.

# Cooking Is Elementary!

**Skill:** Reading a recipe

**Materials needed:**
- a simple no-cook snack recipe similar to the one shown
- a class supply of ingredients and materials for making the recipe
- a marker
- a class supply of paper plates
- a class supply of napkins
- a class supply of hand-sanitizing wipes

**Setting up the center:**
Display the materials at a center.

**Using the center:**
1. A student uses a hand wipe to clean her hands.
2. She follows the recipe step-by-step to create the snack.
3. The student writes her name on a paper plate and places her completed snack on it.
4. She covers her snack with a napkin and places the plate in a designated area until snacktime.

### Ants on a Log

1. Spread peanut butter on a piece of celery.
2. Sprinkle cracker crumbs on top of the peanut butter.
3. Place five raisins on top of the cracker crumbs.

Heather

# Fishy Facts

**Skill:** Locating facts

**Materials needed:**
- nonfiction books about fish
- pencils
- a class supply of large index cards
- a class supply of white paper lunch bags
- markers or crayons
- glue
- scissors
- construction paper scraps
- newspaper or scrap paper
- a supply of yarn
- a hole puncher

### To Make Your Fish

First, decorate the bag to resemble a fish.

Then stuff the bag with sheets of newspaper or scrap paper.

Fish breathe with gills.

**Setting up the center:**
1. Make a set of directions and a sample fish similar to the ones shown.
2. Display the directions, sample, and the materials at a center.

**Using the center:**
1. A student looks through the books to find a fact about fish.
2. The student writes his fact on an index card.
3. He follows the listed directions to make a paper bag fish.
4. Using the hole puncher and a length of yarn, the student attaches his fact to the fish as shown.
5. The student places his completed project in a designated display area.

# Digging for Details

**Skill:** Reading for details

**Materials needed:**
- a supply of index cards
- a supply of stickers or pictures cut from magazines
- glue (for magazine pictures)
- a fine-tipped marker

*I walk on four legs.*

*I have spikes on my back.*

**Setting up the center:**
1. Attach stickers or glue magazine cutouts to half of the index cards.
2. Write on the remaining index cards a set of clues to go with each picture.
3. Program the backs of corresponding picture and clue cards with matching numbers or letters for self-checking. Laminate the cards for durability, if desired.
4. Display the cards at a center.

**Using the center:**
1. A student spreads out the cards on the center surface for easy viewing.
2. She reads each clue card, matching it to a corresponding picture card.
3. When all cards have been matched, she turns them over to check her work.

# Feathered Friends

**Skill:** Reading for details

**Materials needed:**
- a selection of nonfiction books about birds
- a class supply of the booklet pattern on page 43
- crayons or markers
- scissors      • a hole puncher
- a stapler     • a supply of yarn or string

Cardinal
(name of bird)

by ____ Jim
(name)

**Setting up the center:**
1. Make a sample booklet like the one shown.
2. Display the sample and the materials at a center.

**Using the center:**
1. A student looks through the books and chooses a bird to research.
2. He reads to find information describing his bird and then writes or illustrates the information on the appropriate section of the booklet pattern.
3. He cuts apart the completed pattern along the dotted lines.
4. The student stacks the resulting pages in order and staples the booklet together. He then makes a hole at the top of the booklet, threads a length of yarn or string through it, and ties the two ends together.
5. The student hangs his completed project in a designated display area.

# Main Idea in a Nutshell

**Skill:** Identifying main idea

**Materials needed:**
- a selection of short stories
- a class supply of brown construction paper cutouts of the nutshell pattern on page 44
- a class supply of the nutshell form on page 44
- scissors
- glue
- pencils

Book Title: *Armadillo Rodeo*
Author: *Jan Brett*

Main Idea: *An armadillo named Bo follows a pair of red cowboy boots (which he thinks is an armadillo) to the Curly H Ranch. He has all sorts of adventures until his mom comes to take him home.*

Name: *Kara*

**Setting up the center:**
Display the materials at a center.

**Using the center:**
1. A student selects a short story to read.
2. After reading, the student completes the form, telling about her book and its main idea.
3. She cuts out the form and a nutshell pattern and glues them together as shown.
4. The student places her completed project in a designated display area.

# Beginning, Middle, and End Friend

**Skill:** Identifying story sequence

**Materials needed:**
- a selection of books
- a class supply of the pattern and form on page 45
- scissors
- pencils
- glue
- crayons or markers

**Beginning**
Some sheep wake up and pack their gear to go on a hike.

**Middle**
They trot along a hiking trail but get lost.

**End**
They find their trail and head home.

**Setting up the center:**
Display the materials at a center.

**Using the center:**
1. A student selects a book to read.
2. He completes the story information on the form.
3. He cuts out the bear pattern and form. He folds the form along the dashed lines and then glues it to the bear as shown.
4. He writes his name and the title and author of the book on the top flap of the folded strip.
5. The student decorates the bear as desired and places it in a designated display area.

# Book Boxes

**Skill:** Identifying story events

**Materials needed:**
- a selection of students' favorite books
- a class supply of cereal boxes, each with its front panel cut to form a door
- a supply of 9" x 12" sheets of white construction paper
- crayons or markers
- magazines
- scissors
- glue

**Setting up the center:**
Display all the materials at a center.

**Using the center:**
1. A student selects a book to read.
2. After reading, the student decorates a cover on a sheet of construction paper.
3. She cuts out pictures from magazines to represent story details, gluing them onto another sheet of construction paper.
4. The student glues the cover sheet to the outside front panel of the box and the story details sheet to the inside back panel as shown.
5. The student places her completed project in a designated display area.

# Critic's Corner

**Skill:** Writing a story summary

**Materials needed:**
- a selection of students' favorite books
- a class supply of the form on page 46
- scissors
- glue
- pencils
- crayons or markers

**Setting up the center:**
Display all the materials at a center.

**Using the center:**
1. A student selects a book to read.
2. He completes the story form as directed on page 46.
3. The student places his completed project in a designated display area.

# Lists, Lists, Lists

**Skill:** Writing lists

**Materials needed:**
- a sheet of construction paper
- a class supply of the list form on page 47
- pencils
- a timer

**Setting up the center:**
1. Choose several topics for the list, such as pets, groceries, words I can spell, etc. Record the topics on the sheet of construction paper.
2. Display the topics list, forms, pencils, and timer at a center.

**Using the center:**
1. A student takes a form and a pencil. She chooses a topic from the list.
2. She fills in the chosen topic and sets the timer for two minutes.
3. She lists as many items as possible to match the chosen topic.
4. If time allows, she may choose her own topic, set the timer again, and make a list of possible words on the back of her form.

# Acrostic Favorites

**Skills:** Writing poetry, understanding parts of speech

**Materials needed:**
- a plastic jar or container
- slips of paper
- a class supply of blank white paper
- markers or crayons
- a dictionary
- a thesaurus

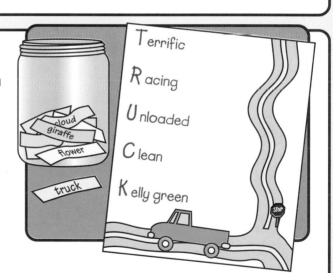

**Setting up the center:**
1. On each slip of paper, write a common noun, such as *truck, flower,* or *giraffe.*
2. Place the labeled slips in the jar.
3. Create a sample poem like the one shown.
4. Display the jar, sample poem, paper, markers or crayons, dictionary, and thesaurus at a center.

**Using the center:**
1. A student draws a slip from the jar.
2. He writes the noun vertically on a sheet of paper.
3. He writes an adjective for each letter of his word, using the dictionary and thesaurus when necessary.
4. He illustrates his poem.
5. If time allows, he may choose another slip from the jar and write another poem.

# Rolling for Words

**Skill:** Understanding parts of speech

**Materials needed:**
- a paper lunch bag
- a set of alphabet cards
- a small tissue box
- a class supply of blank paper
- pencils

**Setting up the center:**
1. Place the alphabet cards in the bag.
2. Create a parts-of-speech cube by labeling each side of the tissue box with a part of speech (see illustration).
3. Display the bag, cube, paper, and pencils at a center.

**Using the center:**
1. A student selects an alphabet card from the bag and prints the letter on a sheet of paper.
2. She rolls the cube and writes on her paper the part of speech facing up.
3. She then writes a word corresponding to both the letter and the part of speech.
4. She completes the activity a total of ten times.
5. If time allows, she may write sentences using the ten words.

# Busy Beavers

**Skill:** Understanding parts of speech

**Materials needed:**
- 10 cutouts of the beaver pattern on page 48
- a permanent marker
- 2 cardboard tubes
- a brown crayon or marker
- 4 paper clips

**Setting up the center:**
1. Program each beaver with a different noun or verb. Indicate on each tail whether the word is a noun or a verb.
2. Color the beavers, if desired.
3. Fold each tail as shown.
4. Label one tube "noun" and the other "verb." Color the tubes to resemble logs.
5. Put a paper clip on the end of each log to prevent rolling. Display the beavers and the logs at a center.

**Using the center:**
1. A student reads the word on each beaver and decides whether it is a noun or a verb.
2. He places each beaver by its corresponding log.
3. After all of the beavers have been placed, he unfolds the tails to check his answers.
4. If time allows, he may write a sentence using each word.

# WORD ROUNDUP

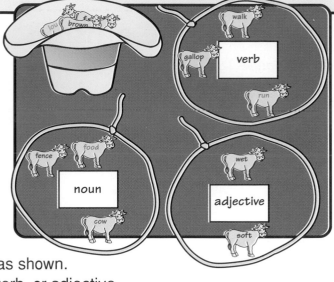

**Skill:** Identifying parts of speech

**Materials needed:**
- 3 index cards
- 20 brown construction paper cutouts of the cow pattern on page 48
- markers
- three 36" lengths of yarn
- a large resealable plastic bag or a cowboy hat

**Setting up the center:**
1. Label each index card with a part of speech as shown.
2. Program the front of each cow with a noun, verb, or adjective.
3. Label the back of each cow with its correct part of speech. Store the cutouts in the bag or hat.
4. Tie the ends of each string to resemble a lasso as shown.
5. Display the cards, hat or bag, and lassos at a center.

**Using the center:**
1. A student picks a cow from the bag or cowboy hat.
2. She reads the word on the cow and determines whether it is a noun, verb, or adjective.
3. She places the cow inside its corresponding lasso.
4. She continues in the same manner until she places all the cows.
5. She then turns over the cows to check her work.

# Hanging Out With Words

**Skill:** Constructing complete sentences

**Materials needed:**
- 5 construction paper cutouts of each clothing pattern on page 49
- 3 index cards
- markers
- a 4' length of clothesline or rope
- a supply of spring clothespins
- a laundry basket
- a class supply of lined paper
- pencils

**Setting up the center:**
1. Program each clothing cutout with a word that corresponds with a part of speech as shown. Color and laminate each cutout, if desired.
2. Program one index card with a period and the remaining cards with the articles "the" and "a."
3. Suspend the clothesline between two chairs. Hang the index cards on the clothesline.
4. Place the clothing cutouts in the laundry basket.
5. Display the clothesline, clothespins, laundry basket, paper, and pencils at a center.

**Using the center:**
1. A student chooses one of the article cards to begin his sentence.
2. He then chooses one of each type of clothing.
3. He clips the index card and clothing to the clothesline to make a complete sentence.
4. He records his sentence on a sheet of paper and repeats the activity until he has formed five sentences.

# Recycled Sentences

**Skill:** Writing complete sentences

**Materials needed:**
- a class supply of favorite books and magazines
- pencils or pens
- a class supply of blank paper
- markers or crayons

**Setting up the center:**
1. Create a sample such as the one shown.
2. Display the materials at a center.

**Using the center:**
1. A student selects a page from a book or magazine.
2. She chooses words from the page to make a complete sentence.
3. She writes her sentence at the bottom of a sheet of paper and then illustrates a picture of it at the top.
4. If time allows, she may write a short story on the back of the sheet using her sentence as a prompt.

*She ran around the meadow.*

# Add-a-Line

**Skill:** Writing complete sentences

**Materials needed:**
- an old weekly planner with pictures, such as the example shown
- pencils or pens

**Setting up the center:**
1. In each Sunday space, write a story starter relating to the corresponding picture.
2. Display the materials at a center.

| | |
|---|---|
| Sunday 27 | Hilda the beekeeper was having a bad day! |
| Monday 28 | First her bees got loose. *Danny* |
| Tuesday 29 | Then the honey dripped out of the hive. *Stevie* |
| Wednesday 30 | Then a bee stung her. *Andy* |
| Thursday 1 | But then she got an idea. *Jose* |
| Friday 2 | |
| Saturday 3 | |

**Using the center:**
1. A student selects a picture in the planner that interests him.
2. He reads the story starter.
3. He writes a sentence and signs his name in the next available space.
4. If time allows, he may choose to add a sentence to another story in the book.
5. A story is complete when each space through the Saturday space is filled by students.

# Easy As Pie

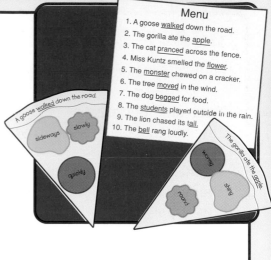

**Skill:** Adding detail to sentences

**Materials needed:**
- a class supply of cutouts of the pizza pattern on page 50
- a variety of construction paper shapes to resemble toppings
- a sheet of construction paper
- a pizza pan
- pencils
- glue

**Setting up the center:**
1. Create a menu of sentences on the sheet of construction paper similar to the ones shown.
2. Underline a noun or action verb in each sentence.
3. Place the topping cutouts in the pizza pan.
4. Display the menu, pizza slices, pizza pan, pencils, and glue at a center.

**Using the center:**
1. A student reads the menu and selects a sentence.
2. She copies the sentence onto the crust of a pizza slice.
3. She writes three adjectives or adverbs for the underlined word, each on a different topping.
4. She glues each topping to her pizza slice.
5. She writes the new sentences on the back of the pizza slices.

---

# Awesome Alliteration

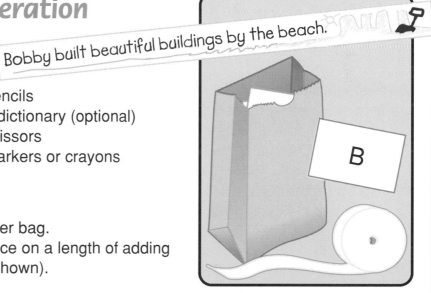

Bobby built beautiful buildings by the beach.

**Skill:** Writing alliterative sentences

**Materials needed:**
- a set of alphabet cards
- a paper lunch bag
- a roll of adding machine tape
- scrap paper
- pencils
- a dictionary (optional)
- scissors
- markers or crayons

**Setting up the center:**
1. Put the alphabet cards in the paper bag.
2. Write a sample alliterative sentence on a length of adding machine tape (see the example shown).
3. Display the materials at a center.

**Using the center:**
1. A student draws a letter from the bag.
2. He writes words that begin with the chosen letter on a sheet of paper; then he writes several sentences using the words.
3. He copies his favorite alliterative sentence onto the adding machine tape, unrolling it as he writes, and then illustrates it.
4. He cuts off his sentence and posts his strip in a designated area.

# BEACH BALL PUNCTUATION

**Skill:** Punctuating sentences

**Materials needed:**
- an inflated beach ball
- a permanent marker
- a class supply of lined paper
- pencils

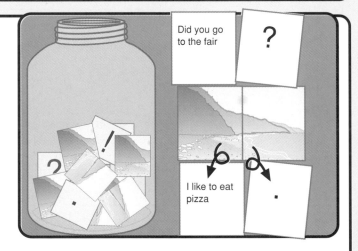

**Setting up the center:**
1. Use the permanent marker to label each section of the ball with a punctuation mark as shown.
2. Display the beach ball, paper, and pencils at a center.

**Using the center:**
1. A student gently tosses the ball into the air and catches it.
2. She takes note of the punctuation mark in the section under her right thumb.
3. She writes a sentence on a sheet of paper to correspond with the punctuation mark.
4. She repeats the activity until she has written five to ten sentences.

# Postcard Puzzles

**Skill:** Punctuating sentences

**Materials needed:**
- 3 sets of 5 matching postcards (15 postcards)
- 1 fine-tipped marker
- 1 plastic jar or container

**Setting up the center:**
1. Cut one set of postcards in half widthwise.
2. Program the left side of each card with a declarative sentence and the right side with a period.
3. Program the remaining two sets using exclamatory and interrogative sentences and matching punctuation marks.
4. Place the cards in a jar and display the jar at a center.

**Using the center:**
1. A student removes the contents of the jar.
2. He places each card writing side up.
3. He reads the sentence on each card and places the matching punctuation card next to it.
4. He turns over the postcards to check his work.

# May I Take a Message?

**Skills:** Creative writing, filling out forms

**Materials needed:**
- a selection of picture books
- a telephone (real or toy)
- a telephone memo pad
- pencils or pens

**Setting up the center:**
Display the materials at a center.

**Using the center:**
1. A student selects a favorite character from one of the books.
2. She pretends that she receives a phone call from the character and needs to take a message.
3. She fills out the form, recording the name of the character, the date of the call, the message, and whom the message is for.
4. If time allows, she may continue taking messages from her favorite characters.

**MEMO**

Date: _Sept. 2_
To: _Clayton_
From: _Franklin_
Message:
_____Do you have a_____
_____secret club I_____
_____could join?_____
_____
Signed _Emily Jane_

# Mailing Mechanics

**Skill:** Addressing an envelope

**Materials needed:**
- glue
- a 9" x 12" sheet of construction paper
- a sheet of red construction paper
- a brad
- a shoebox

- an inexpensive address book
- a class supply of blank paper
- colored pencils or markers
- square stickers to resemble stamps

ADDRESS BOOK

Jade Popp
4993 Main St.
Allentown, PA 19540

Douglass Bryant
3000 Evergreen Lane
Slatington, PA 18080

**Setting up the center:**
1. Use the first five materials to decorate the shoebox to resemble a mailbox as shown.
2. Write imaginary addresses in the address book.
3. Cut each sheet of blank paper in half widthwise to create "envelopes."
4. Display the mailbox, address book, envelopes, pencils, or markers, and stickers at a center.

**Using the center:**
1. A student selects an address from the address book and prints it in the appropriate place on a paper envelope.
2. He prints his own address in the upper left-hand corner of the envelope.
3. He adds a stamp and then places the envelope in the mailbox.
4. If time allows, he may address and mail additional letters.

# TOOTH TALES

**Skill:** Writing a friendly letter

**Materials needed:**
- a copy of *The Lost Tooth Club* by Arden Johnson (Tricycle Press, 1998)
- a shirt box or a shoebox
- markers
- a class supply of lined paper
- pencils

Mail to Arden Johnson

Rose Reed
Sunnydale School
100 West Ave.
Allentown, PA
00005

Dear Arden,

Thank you for inviting me to write you a letter.

I lost my first tooth last year when I was eating popcorn at the movies. My tooth was lost.

Write soon,

Rose

**Setting up the center:**
1. Label the front of the box similarly to the one shown.
2. Create a sample friendly letter.
3. Display the book, box, sample letter, pencils, paper, and markers at a center.

**Using the center:**
1. A student reads the book or follows along as you read the book aloud.
2. She writes a friendly letter to the author explaining how her first tooth was lost.
3. She illustrates her letter and places it in the box.
4. After each child has written a letter, send them to the author or make a class book.

# Advice Is Nice!

**Skill:** Writing a friendly letter

**Materials needed:**
- a sheet of chart paper
- markers
- an assortment of writing paper (postcards, notecards, stationery, etc.)
- pencils

Dear 3 Pigs,
Brick is your best choice for building and it keps most wolves out.
Love,
Ian

### Our Favorite Stories

| | |
|---|---|
| Three Little Pigs | wolf, 3 pigs |
| Arthur's Computer Disaster | Arthur, D. W., Buster, the Brain |
| Junie B. Jones Is Not a Cook | Junie B. Jones, Mrs., Lucille, William, Grace, Principal, grampa Miller |
| Too Many Pumpkins | Rebecca Estelle, Esmeralda (her cat), truck driver |

Dear pumpkin truck driver,
Please drive safely so that you don't lose any more pumpkins. Maybe you could hire someone to sit in the back of your truck.
Love,
Alan

**Setting up the center:**
1. Make a class list of favorite stories and their corresponding characters on the sheet of chart paper.
2. Display the list, assortment of paper, and pencils at a center.

**Using the center:**
1. A student chooses a story and corresponding character from the list.
2. He writes a letter to the character, giving advice on how to solve a problem or change the outcome of a story event. He adds an illustration, if desired.
3. If time allows, he may write another letter of advice to a different character.

# Silly Stories

**Skill:** Creative writing

**Materials needed:**
- 12 index cards
- a marker
- 2 paper lunch bags
- a class supply of lined paper
- pencils

**Setting up the center:**
1. Program each paper bag and two sets of index cards as shown.
2. Put each set of cards into its corresponding bag.
3. Display the bags, paper, and pencils at a center.

**Using the center:**
1. A student selects one card from each bag to create a story title.
2. She writes the title at the top of a sheet of paper.
3. She writes a story to correspond with the title.
4. If time allows, she may illustrate her story.

# Picnic Stories

**Skill:** Creative writing

**Materials needed:**
- 5 large resealable bags
- a picnic basket
- 15 small items
- a class supply of lined paper
- a class supply of drawing paper
- pencils
- crayons or markers

**Setting up the center:**
1. Place three items in each resealable bag.
2. Seal the bags and put them in the picnic basket.
3. Display the basket, paper, pencils, and crayons or markers at a center.

**Using the center:**
1. A student chooses a bag from the picnic basket.
2. He writes a story on lined paper using the three items.
3. He illustrates his story on a sheet of drawing paper.
4. He returns the sealed bag of items to the picnic basket.
5. If time allows, he may pick another bag from the basket and write another story.

# Stamp-a-Story

**Skills:** Creative writing, vocabulary building

**Materials needed:**
- a variety of rubber stamps (or stickers)
- several different-colored ink pads
- a list of vocabulary or spelling words
- a class supply of blank paper
- pencils
- a highlighter

**Setting up the center:**
   Display the materials at a center.

**Using the center:**
1. A student chooses five words from the vocabulary list and prints them on a sheet of paper.
2. She writes a rebus story using the words and the stamps.
3. She highlights each vocabulary word that she used in the story.
4. If time allows, she may write a story starter on another sheet of paper so that her classmates can add to it when they visit the center.

It was a ☀ day.
I saw a beetle
eating some leaves. She
then crawled away to a
tree. She was ☺.

by
Athena

**Vocabulary List**

| | |
|---|---|
| insect | digging |
| ladybug | dug |
| cricket | eating |
| beetle | ate |
| butterfly | crawled |
| tree | crawling |
| leaves | flying |
| flower | flew |
| | hiding |
| | hid |

# Notepad Creations

**Skill:** Creative writing

**Materials needed:**
- a variety of notepad sheets (see examples shown)
- a supply of lined paper
- glue
- pencils
- markers

**Setting up the center:**
   Display the materials at a center.

**Using the center:**
1. A student selects a notepad sheet.
2. He glues the notepad sheet to the top portion of a sheet of paper.
3. He writes a corresponding story and a title.
4. If time allows, he may add illustrations to the notepad sheet.

My Ride Home

One day my bus forgot to
take me home. I was alseep. My
driver woke me up and took
me home.

by
Darren

# Fishing for Stories

**Skill:** Creative writing

**Materials needed:**
- a permanent marker
- 4 plastic fishbowls or other bowls
- 28 construction paper fish
- a class supply of lined paper
- pencils

**Setting up the center:**
1. Label each bowl with a different story element as shown.
2. Label seven fish with examples of specific story elements to correspond with each bowl (see illustration).
3. Store the fish in their matching bowls.
4. Display the bowls, paper, and pencils at a center.

**Using the center:**
1. A student draws a fish from each bowl.
2. She writes a story using the story elements on the fish.
3. If time allows, she may illustrate her story on the back of her paper.

# Shapes Make Our World

**Skill:** Creative writing

**Materials needed:**
- a supply of different-colored construction paper shapes
- glue
- a class supply of lined paper
- crayons
- pencils

**Setting up the center:**
Display the materials at a center.

**Using the center:**
1. A student selects a shape and glues it to the top portion of a sheet of paper.
2. He draws a picture, including the shape as part of the drawing.
3. He writes a story on the bottom half of the paper to correspond with his drawing.
4. If time allows, he may choose another shape and write another story.

# Story on a Stick

**Skill:** Creative writing

**Materials needed:**
- 5 plastic cups
- a supply of craft sticks
- a fine-tipped permanent marker
- a class supply of lined paper
- pencils

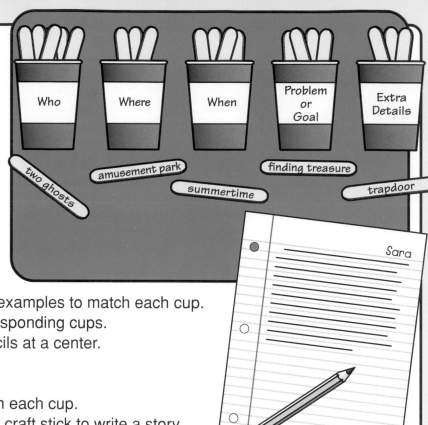

**Setting up the center:**
1. Label each cup as shown.
2. Program several craft sticks with examples to match each cup.
3. Store the craft sticks in their corresponding cups.
4. Display the cups, paper, and pencils at a center.

**Using the center:**
1. A student selects a craft stick from each cup.
2. She uses the information on each craft stick to write a story.
3. If time allows, she may illustrate her story.

# Hot off the Press

**Skill:** Writing story details

**Materials needed:**
- a supply of light-colored construction paper
- markers
- scissors
- newspapers
- glue
- pencils

**Newspaper Story Details**

Who is in the story?
Where does the story take place?
When does the story take place?
What is happening in the story?
Why or how did it happen?

**New Golf Restaurant Is a Hit!**
*Reported by Victor*

A golf restaurant opened in town yesterday. Golfers talked about golf and ate golf burgers made of meatballs. Golf ball soup was also very popular!

**Setting up the center:**
1. Create a story detail chart on a sheet of construction paper as shown.
2. Cut out a variety of newspaper pictures. Glue each picture to a sheet of construction paper.
3. Display the chart, construction-paper pictures, construction paper, glue, and pencils at a center.

**Using the center:**
1. A student selects a newspaper picture.
2. He pretends to be a reporter and writes a title and a short story to correspond with the picture.
3. If desired, after each student completes a page, bind the pages together to make a class newspaper.

# Writing Makes Sense

**Skill:** Writing descriptive details

**Materials needed:**
- a large resealable plastic bag
- a permanent marker
- a supply of index cards
- a sheet of construction paper
- a class supply of lined paper
- pencils

barber shop

Juanita
I see chairs that go up and down, combs, magazines, and a cash register. I hear scissors cutting, a buzzing sound, and people talking.

What do you...
see?
hear?
smell?
taste?
touch?

Setting
a circus

**Setting up the center:**
1. Use the permanent marker to label the plastic bag as shown.
2. Program each index card with a different setting. Store the cards in the bag.
3. Make a construction paper chart similar to the one shown.
4. Display the bag, chart, paper, and pencils at a center.

**Using the center:**
1. A student selects a setting card from the bag.
2. She writes details about the setting using the chart as a guide.
3. If time allows, she may select another setting card and repeat the activity.

# Three-Minute Poems

**Skill:** Writing poetry

**Materials needed:**
- a supply of old magazines
- scissors
- a class supply of construction paper
- a timer
- glue
- pencils
- markers or crayons

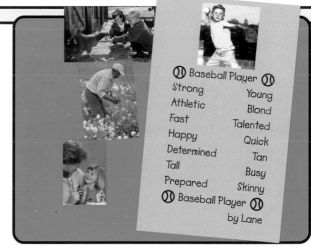

⚾ Baseball Player ⚾
Strong          Young
Athletic        Blond
Fast            Talented
Happy           Quick
Determined      Tan
Tall            Busy
Prepared        Skinny
⚾ Baseball Player ⚾
              by Lane

**Setting up the center:**
1. Cut out a variety of magazine pictures.
2. Cut each sheet of construction paper in half lengthwise.
3. Display the pictures, paper, timer, glue, pencils, and crayons or markers at a center.

**Using the center:**
1. A student selects a magazine picture and glues it to the top of a half sheet of construction paper.
2. He writes a corresponding title beneath the picture.
3. To create his poem, he sets the timer for three minutes and writes as many adjectives as he can to describe the picture.
4. When the timer rings, he writes the title at the bottom of his paper and adds decorative details to finish the poem.
5. If time allows, he may choose another picture and write another poem.

# My Shopping Lists

1. _____

2. _____

3. _____

4. _____

5. _____

1. _____

2. _____

3. _____

4. _____

5. _____

1. _____

2. _____

3. _____

4. _____

5. _____

1. _____

2. _____

3. _____

4. _____

5. _____

**Note to the teacher:** Use with "Shopping With 'Alpha-Betty'" on page 7.

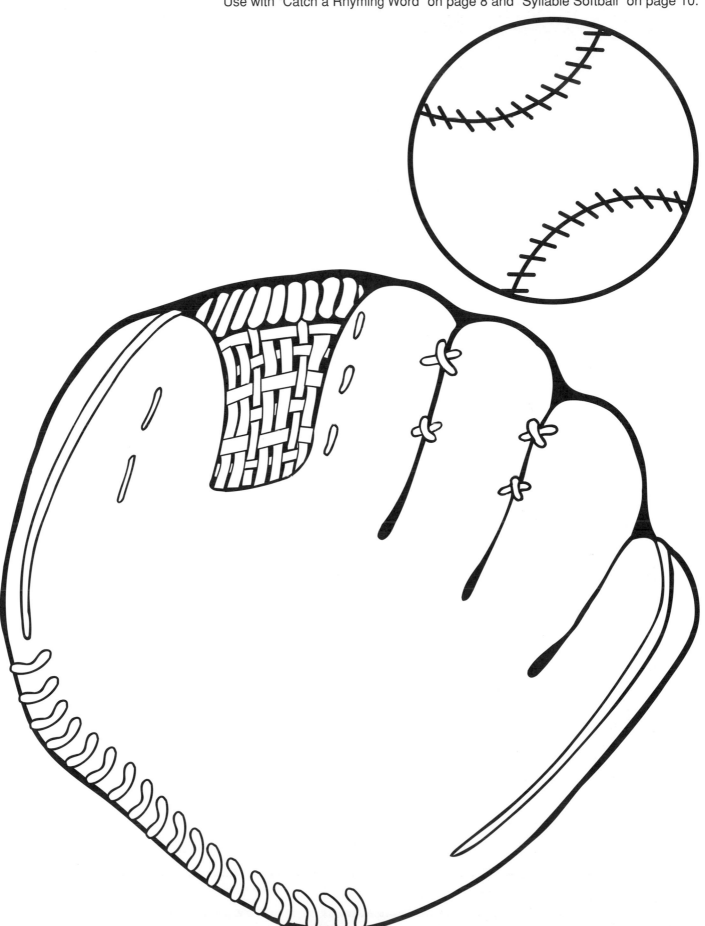

# Caterpillar Patterns
Use with "Lots of Legs" on page 9.

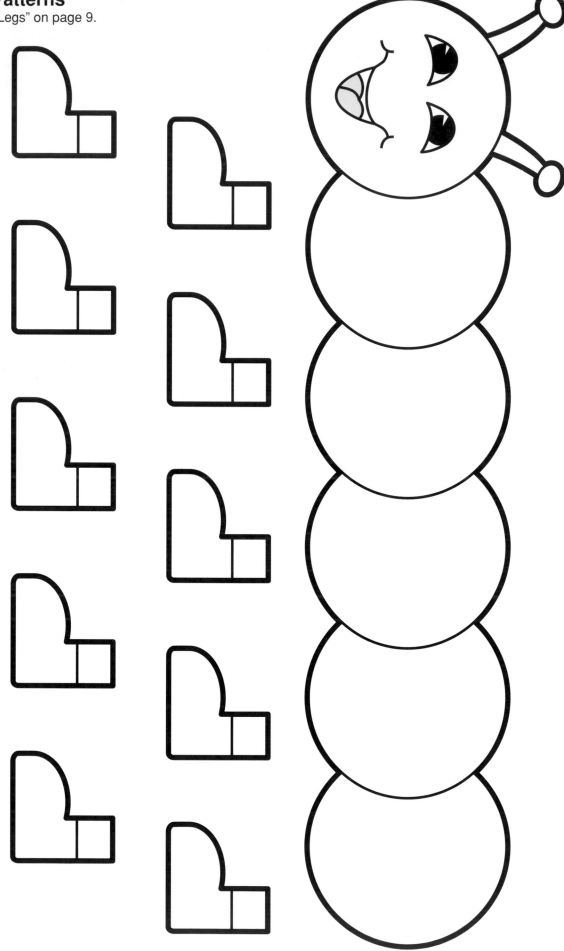

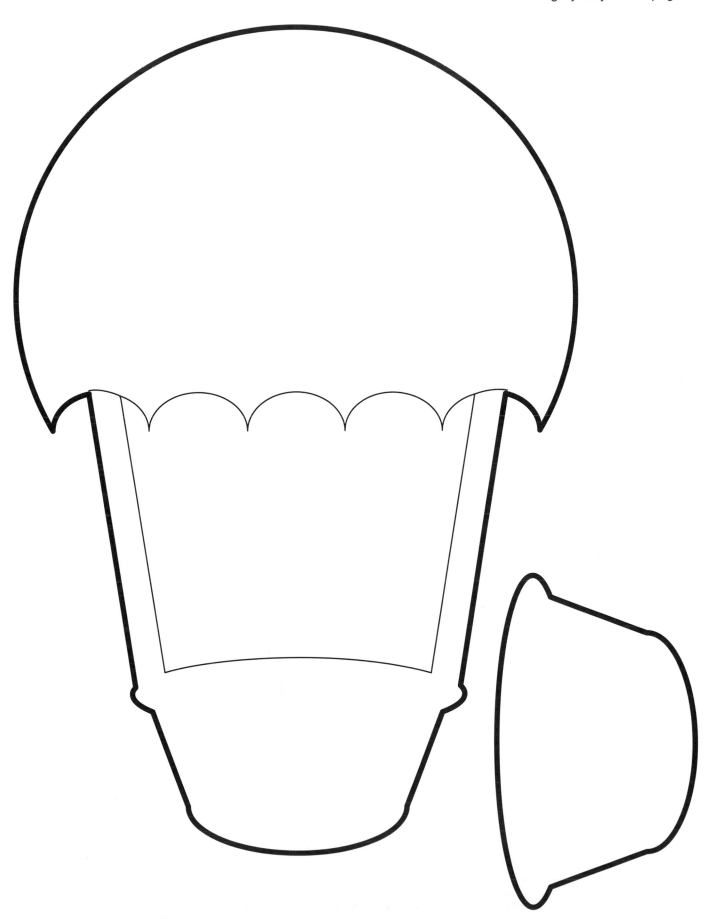

# Train and Track Patterns

Use with "On Track With Contractions" on page 15.

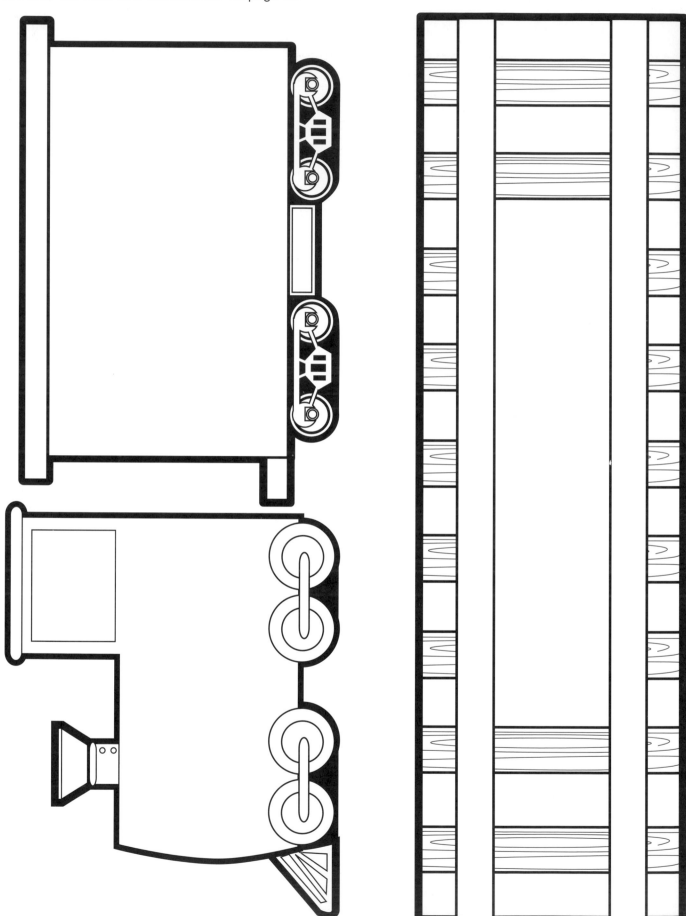

 # Possessive or Contraction?

| Word Found | Possessive or Contraction? | What It Means |
|---|---|---|
|  |  |  |
|  |  |  |
|  |  |  |
|  |  |  |
|  |  |  |
|  |  |  |
|  |  |  |
|  |  |  |
|  |  |  |
|  |  |  |

**Note to the teacher:** Use with "Possessive or Contraction?" on page 15.

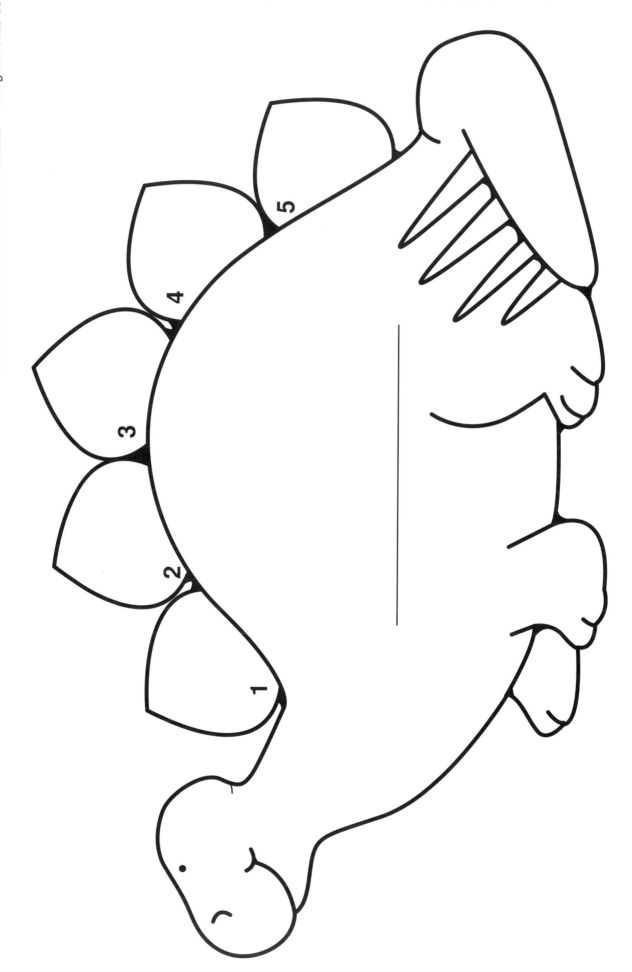

**Note to the teacher:** Use with "Thesaur-o-saurus" on page 16.

**Booklet Pattern**

Use with "Feathered Friends" on page 20.

**Directions:**
1. Draw a picture of your bird in the circle.
2. Write or illustrate the information in each box.
3. Cut on the dotted lines.
4. Staple the pages in order.
5. Hole-punch the top; then loop and tie yarn or string through the hole.

_____
(name of bird)

by _____
(name)

4

3

**Food**

**Habitat**

2

1

**Eggs**

**Nest**

# Nutshell Pattern and Form

Use with "Main Idea in a Nutshell" on page 21.

**Book Title:** _____

**Author:** _____

**Main Idea:** _____

_____

_____

_____

_____

**Name:** _____

## Bear Pattern and Form
Use with "Beginning, Middle, and End Friend" on page 21.

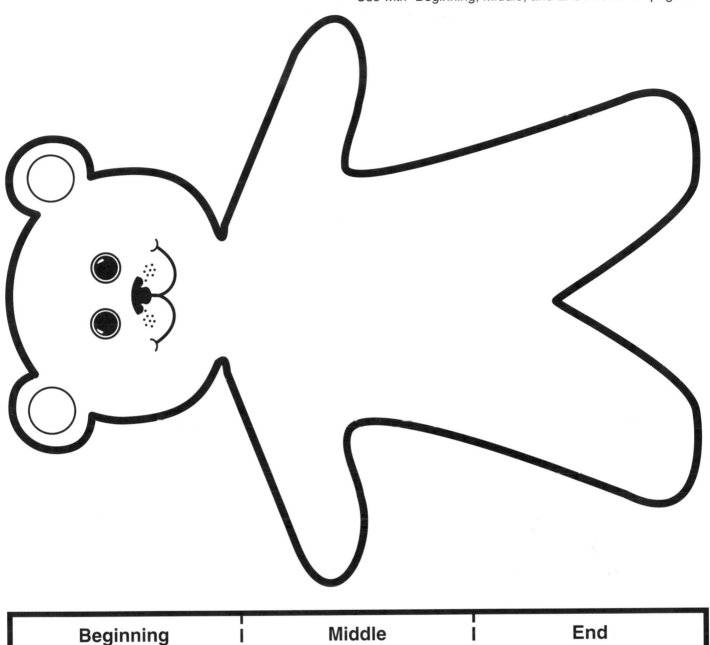

| Beginning | Middle | End |
|-----------|--------|-----|
|           |        |     |

45

Name _____   *Writing a story summary*

# Critic's Corner

**Directions:**
1. Complete each section.
2. Cut out the shape along the bold lines.
3. Fold along the dashed lines.
4. Glue the sides together where shown.

(glue)

(fold)

**Title:** _____

**Author:** _____

(fold)

What is this story about?

_____
_____
_____
_____
_____

Here is a picture of my favorite part.

(fold)

_____
Name

Would you tell others to read this book? Why or why not?

**Note to the teacher:** Use with "Critic's Corner" on page 22.

Name _____

# My List of

_____
(topic)

1. _____

2. _____

3. _____

4. _____

5. _____

6. _____

7. _____

8. _____

9. _____

10. _____

Name _____

# My List of

_____
(topic)

1. _____

2. _____

3. _____

4. _____

5. _____

6. _____

7. _____

8. _____

9. _____

10. _____

**Note to the teacher:** Use with "List, Lists, Lists" on page 23.

# Beaver Pattern
Use with "Busy Beavers" on page 24.

# Cow Pattern
Use with "Word Roundup" on page 25.

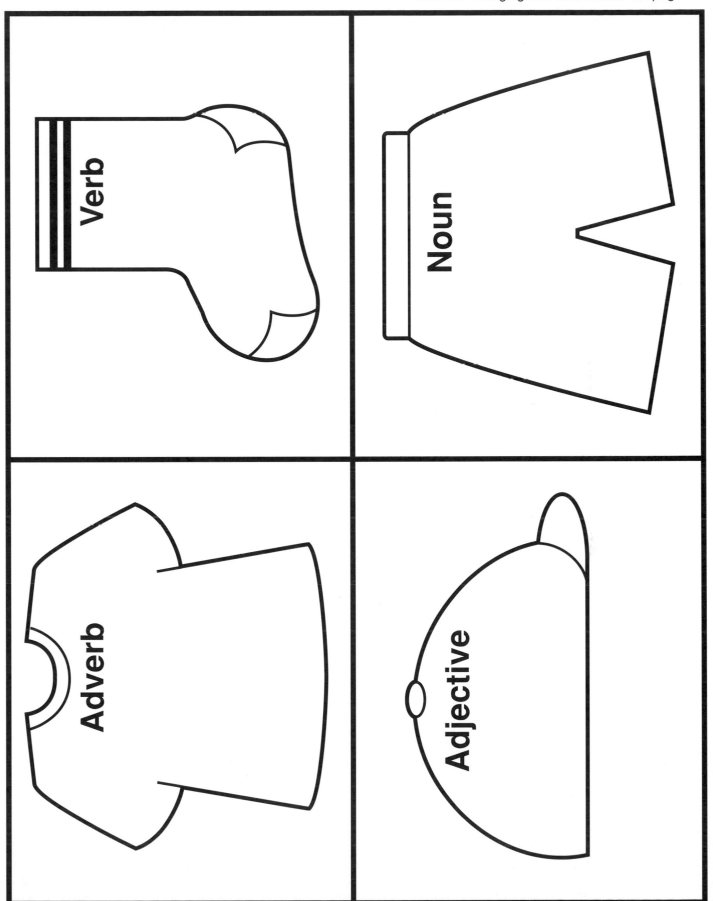

# Pizza Patterns
Use with "Easy As Pie" on page 27.

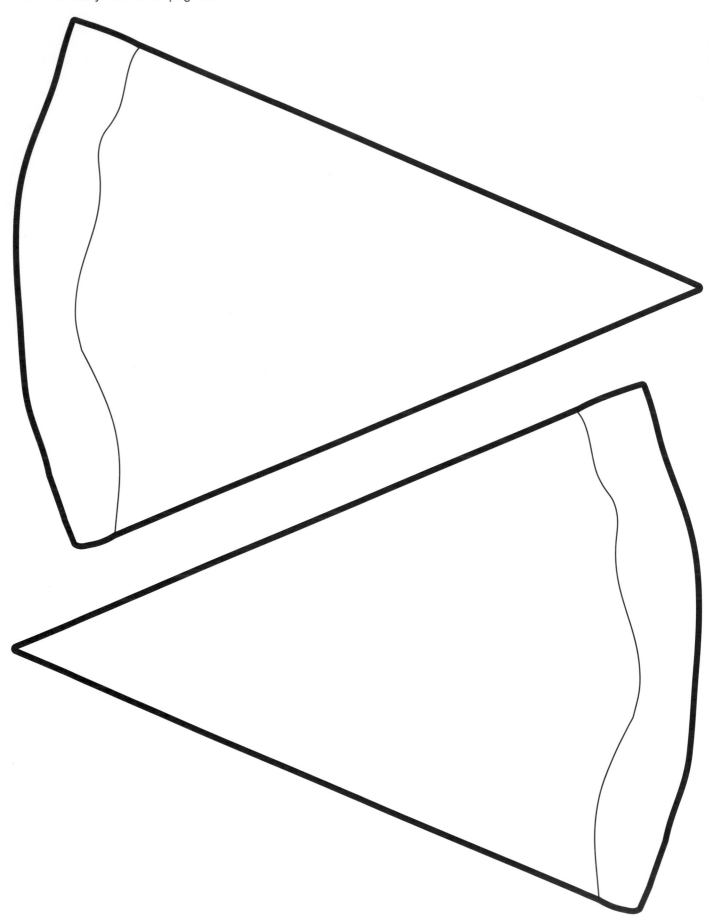

# Math

# Step Into Skip-Counting

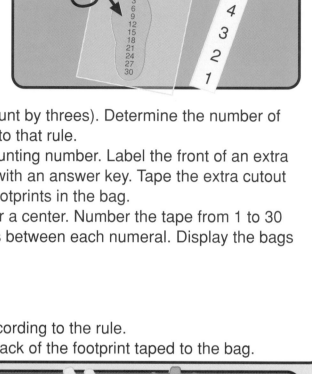

**Skill:** Skip-counting

**Materials needed:**
- a supply of 3" construction paper footprint cutouts
- a permanent marker
- a supply of quart-sized resealable bags
- an 8' length of 2" masking tape
- a ruler

**Setting up the center:**
1. Identify a rule for skip-counting (for example, count by threes). Determine the number of footprints needed to skip-count to 30 according to that rule.
2. Label each footprint with an appropriate skip-counting number. Label the front of an extra cutout with the skip-counting rule and the back with an answer key. Tape the extra cutout to the inside of the bag and put the remaining footprints in the bag.
3. Tape the length of masking tape to the floor near a center. Number the tape from 1 to 30 with the permanent marker, leaving three inches between each numeral. Display the bags at the center.

**Using the center:**
1. A student selects a bag and reads the rule.
2. She places the footprints on the number line according to the rule.
3. The student checks her work by looking at the back of the footprint taped to the bag.

# Five-Finger Fun

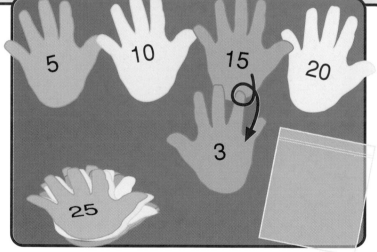

**Skill:** Skip-counting by fives

**Materials needed:**
- 20 hand cutouts
- markers
- a resealable plastic bag

**Setting up the center:**
1. Number the hand cutouts by fives from 5 to 100. Number the backs of the cutouts from 1 to 20 for self-checking. (For a variation, use ten pairs of foot cutouts. Number the cutout pairs by tens from 10 to 100. Number the backs of the cutouts 1–10 for self-checking.)
2. Place the cutouts in a resealable plastic bag. Display the bag at a center.

**Using the center:**
1. A student removes the cutouts from the bag.
2. He looks at the numbers on the fronts of the cutouts and arranges them in sequential order.
3. The student looks at the backs of the cutouts to check his work.

# Sea-Creature Sequencing

**Skill:** Sequencing

**Materials needed:**
- an empty coffee can
- blue Con-Tact® paper
- assorted sea-creature cutouts
- permanent markers
- pencils
- a class supply of blank paper

**Setting up the center:**
1. Cover the coffee can with blue Con-Tact® paper.
2. Use the markers to decorate the can with an ocean scene and to label each cutout with a different number as desired.
3. Create an answer key on a cutout showing the numbers in correct order.
4. Place the cutouts and the answer key in the can. Display the can, paper, and pencils at a center.

**Using the center:**
1. A student removes the cutouts and arranges them in sequential order.
2. She writes the numbers on her paper and then checks her work using the answer key.

# What's Next?

**Skill:** Sequencing

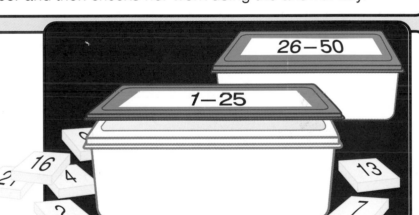

**Materials needed:**
- 100 ceramic tiles
- a permanent marker
- 4 empty diaper wipe containers

**Setting up the center:**
1. Use a permanent marker to label each tile with a different number from 1 to 100.
2. Divide the tiles into four groups: 1–25, 26–50, 51–75, and 76–100.
3. Place each group of tiles in a separate container. Label each container with a different number group.
4. Display the containers at a center.

**Using the center:**
1. A student chooses a container and removes the tiles.
2. He arranges the tiles in numerical order or in reverse numerical order, as desired.
3. If time allows, he may mix up the tiles and then arrange them in desired numerical patterns (for example, 2, 4, 6… or 5, 10, 15…).

# Come to Order!

**Skill:** Sequencing

**Materials needed:**
- 10 index cards
- an envelope, laminated for durability, if desired
- a hundreds chart
- markers
- a supply of seasonal stickers

**Setting up the center:**
1. Label one index card with a number between 1 and 100. Label each remaining card with the nine numbers that follow the first number.
2. Embellish the cards with seasonal stickers.
3. Shuffle the cards and place them in the envelope.
4. If desired, make additional sets of cards labeled with different number patterns. Label each envelope with a different sticker and place a card set in it.
5. Display the envelope and hundreds chart at a center.

**Using the center:**
1. A student takes the cards out of the envelope.
2. She places the cards in sequential order and then checks her work by comparing her answers to the hundreds chart.

# CLOWNING AROUND

**Skill:** Identifying ordinal numbers

**Materials needed:**
- a large, plain index card
- 10 small empty Pringles® cans
- 10 cutouts of the clown pattern on page 83
- 10 cutouts of the award pattern on page 83
- markers
- glue

**CLUE CARD**

The green clown came in sixth place.

The gray clown came in eighth place.

The yellow clown came in third place.

The red clown came in second place.

The black clown came in fifth place.

The purple clown came in tenth place.

The blue clown came in first place.

The pink clown came in fourth place.

The orange clown came in ninth place.

The brown clown came in seventh place.

**Setting up the center:**
1. Make a clue card like the one shown. Make an answer key on the back of the card by drawing colored dots in the order described on the card.
2. Color each clown cutout according to the colors listed on the clue card. Glue each clown on a can.
3. Label each award with an ordinal number or word name from first to tenth.

**Using the center:**
1. A student places the awards in numerical order.
2. He reads the clues on the clue card. He determines the order of each clown can and places it behind the appropriate award.
3. He checks his work using the answer key on the back of the clue card.

# Who's First?

**Skill:** Using ordinal numbers

**Materials needed:**
- ten 2" x 2" construction paper squares
- markers
- 10 decorative stickers
- a 25" sentence strip
- an envelope, laminated for durability, if desired

**Setting up the center:**
1. Label each square with an ordinal number or word name from first to tenth.
2. Place the stickers on the sentence strip so that they are evenly spaced. Write the numbers in correct order on the back of the strip. Laminate the strip for durability, if desired.
3. Place the squares and the sentence strip in the envelope.
4. Display the envelope at a center.

**Using the center:**
1. A student removes the strip from the envelope.
2. In turn, she removes each square from the envelope. She reads the ordinal number and places it below the appropriate sticker.
3. She checks her work using the answer key on the back of the strip.

# A FEW ODD CRAYONS

**Skill:** Identifying odd and even numbers

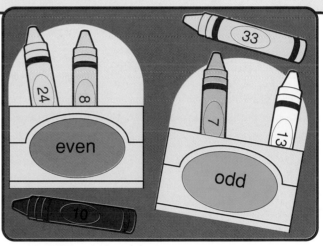

**Materials needed:**
- 2 cutouts of the crayon box pattern on page 84
- 10 cutouts of the crayon pattern on page 84
- clear tape
- crayons
- a large resealable plastic bag

**Setting up the center:**
1. Fold each crayon box cutout along the dotted line and then tape each box along its sides. Label one box "odd" and the other "even." Color the boxes.
2. Write a different number on each crayon cutout. Color each crayon a different color.
3. Label the back of each box with the numbers that correspond to the correct crayons.
4. Place the crayon boxes and crayons in a resealable plastic bag and then display the bag at a center.

**Using the center:**
1. A student removes the crayon boxes and crayons from the bag.
2. He reads the number on each crayon, determining if it is odd or even. He places the crayon in the appropriate box.
3. He turns over the crayon boxes to check his work.

# Sorting Chips

**Skill:** Identifying odd and even numbers

**Materials needed:**
- 2 empty Pringles® cans with lids
- two 9" x 12" sheets of construction paper
- tape
- a permanent marker
- 10 oval construction paper cutouts
- a resealable plastic bag

**Setting up the center:**
1. Cover each can with construction paper. Label the lid of one can "odd" and the other "even."
2. Write a different number from 1 to 10 on each oval cutout, or "chip."
3. Write the numbers that correspond to the correct chips on the bottom of each can.
4. Place the chips in the resealable bag. Display the bag and cans at a center.

**Using the center:**
1. A student removes each lid, placing it near the can.
2. She removes each chip from the bag, reads the number, and places it in the appropriate can.
3. She checks her work by comparing her chips to the numbers on the bottom of each can.

# What's the Scoop?

**Skill:** Identifying place value

**Materials needed:**
- a supply of cutouts of the ice-cream scoop pattern on page 83
- 10 cutouts of the ice-cream cone pattern on page 83
- markers
- a resealable plastic bag

**Setting up the center:**
1. Program each cone cutout with a three-digit number. Color the cones.
2. On the back of each cone, write an expanded-notation sentence showing the values of the numbers on the front (for example, 367 = 300 + 60 + 7).
3. Program each scoop with a different number value that corresponds to the values in an expanded-notation sentence.
4. Place the cones and scoops in the resealable plastic bag. Display the bag at a center.

**Using the center:**
1. A student removes the cones and scoops from the bag. He reads the number on each cone. He identifies the scoops with the corresponding expanded-notation values and uses them to build a triple-dip cone.
2. He flips the cones over to check his work.

# PLACE-VALUE POPCORN

**Skill:** Comparing and ordering numbers

**Materials needed:**
- an empty popcorn bucket
- 10 popcorn-shaped cutouts
- markers
- a class supply of lined paper
- pencils

**Setting up the center:**
1. Label each popcorn cutout with a different number from 0 to 9.
2. Place the cutouts in the bucket, and then display the bucket, paper, and pencils at a center.

**Using the center:**
1. A student removes three popcorn cutouts from the bucket. She uses the numbers to make three different three-digit numbers. She writes the numbers on a sheet of paper.
2. The student compares the numbers and then puts them in order from least to greatest.
3. If time allows, she may serve herself another helping of popcorn.

# High, Low, Three in a Row

**Skill:** Identifying place value

**Materials needed:**
- a deck of playing cards, with face cards and tens removed
- a class supply of the cards form on page 85
- pencils

**Setting up the center:**
Display the materials at a center.

| ♠ High, Low, ♥ | | |
| ♦ Three in a Row ♣ | | |

| My 3 cards | High | Low |
|---|---|---|
| 3  6  5 | 653 | 356 |
|  |  |  |
|  |  |  |
|  |  |  |
|  |  |  |
|  |  |  |
|  |  |  |

Name __Tyler__

**Using the center:**
1. A student shuffles the cards. He draws three cards and records the numbers in the appropriate columns on the form.
2. He arranges the cards to make the highest possible three-digit number and then records the number in the appropriate column.
3. He rearranges the cards to make the lowest possible three-digit number and then records the number in the appropriate column.
4. He draws three more cards and continues in the same manner for up to six additional rounds.

# Caterpillar Comparisons

**Skill:** Comparing numbers

Caterpillar Comparisons

**Materials needed:**
- markers
- a 9" x 12" sheet of construction paper
- 23 two-inch squares of paper
- a resealable plastic bag
- a class supply of blank paper
- pencils

**Setting up the center:**
1. Draw a caterpillar on the sheet of construction paper and add decorative details as shown. Include three two-inch square body segments.
2. Program three paper squares with a different comparison symbol (<, >, or =) and each remaining square with a number from 0 to 9.
3. Store the squares in different resealable bags. Display the caterpillar, bags, pencils, and paper at a center.

**Using the center:**
1. A student removes the squares from the bag. She places the number squares facedown on the playing surface. She draws one number and places it in the first body segment and then draws another number and places it in the third body segment.
2. She determines which comparison symbol to use and places it between the two numbers.
3. She copies the number sentence on her paper. She continues in the same manner until she has written ten number sentences.

# Fraction Folder

**Skill:** Reading mixed numbers

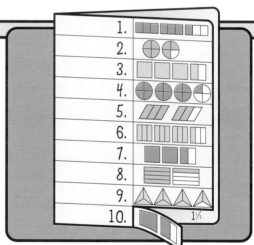

**Materials needed:**
- a manila file folder
- scissors
- markers
- a class supply of blank paper
- pencils

**Setting up the center:**
1. Mark a dividing line down the middle of the file folder. Cut ten equal-sized sections along the right-hand edge of the folder, stopping at the dividing line as shown. (Cut through the top thickness only.) Number each section to the left of the dividing line.
2. On each section, draw a set of shapes that represents a different mixed number.
3. Fold each section on the dividing line to create a flap. Lift each flap and write the depicted mixed number in the space below the flap as shown.
4. Display the folder, paper, and pencils at a center.

**Using the center:**
1. The student numbers a sheet of paper from 1 to 10.
2. He looks at the picture on each flap and writes the mixed number it represents.
3. He lifts the flaps to check his work.

# Pizza...Count Me In!

**Skill:** Solving addition facts

**Materials needed:**
- a supply of index cards
- markers
- a rubber band
- a supply of construction paper cutouts of the pizza pattern on page 86
- a supply of ³/₄" red self-adhesive dots
- an empty pizza box
- pencils

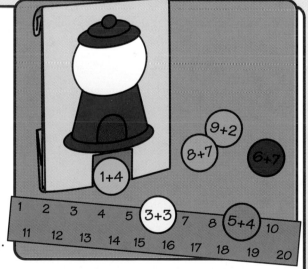

**Setting up the center:**
1. Program each index card with an addition fact. Wrap a rubber band around the cards to hold them together.
2. Place the cards, cutouts, and self-adhesive dots in an empty pizza box. Display the box at a center.

**Using the center:**
1. A student chooses an index card and reads the addition fact.
2. She then writes the addition fact and its answer on the crust of a pizza cutout.
3. The student places that number of pepperoni (self-adhesive dots) on the cutout or slice. She places her completed pizza slice in the box.
4. If time allows, she may choose another index card and help herself to another slice of pizza.

# Gumball Math

**Skill:** Solving addition and subtraction facts

**Materials needed:**
- a paper lunch bag
- scissors
- markers
- a copy of the gumball machine pattern on page 86
- glue
- ten 1¹/₂" construction paper circles
- a sentence strip numbered 1–20 as shown

**Setting up the center:**
1. Cut a two-inch opening along the bottom of the bag.
2. Program the back of the bag with ten addition and subtraction facts and their answers.
3. Color and cut out the gumball machine pattern. Glue it to the front of the bag.
4. Write each fact from the back of the bag on a separate paper circle. Place the paper circles inside the bag.
5. Display the bag and sentence strip at a center.

**Using the center:**
1. A student shakes the bag to get a gumball (paper circle). He reads the fact and then places the gumball atop the correct answer on the sentence strip.
2. He repeats the activity until each gumball is dispensed.
3. After placing all of his gumballs, he looks at the back of the bag to check his work.

# Muffin Math

**Skill:** Solving addition and subtraction facts

**Materials needed:**
- 12 paper muffin-tin liners
- a black marker
- 12 two-inch paper circles
- a muffin tin
- a chef's hat (optional)

**Setting up the center:**
1. Program the inside bottom of each muffin-tin liner with a desired addition or subtraction fact as shown.
2. Write the answer for each fact on a paper circle.
3. Tape each paper circle in a muffin-tin cup.
4. Display the muffin tin, liners, and chef's hat at a center.

**Using the center:**
1. A student chooses a muffin-tin liner and reads the fact. (If desired, she may wear the chef's hat.)
2. She places the liner into the muffin-tin cup that has the correct answer.
3. The student repeats the activity with the remaining facts.

# Lucky Numbers

**Skill:** Solving addition facts

**Materials needed:**
- 11 index cards
- a marker
- a class supply of the "Lucky Numbers" form on page 87
- pencils
- a pair of dice (or number cubes)
- a computer mouse pad (optional)

**Setting up the center:**
1. Label the index cards with numerals from 2 to 12.
2. Display the cards, forms, pencils, dice, and pad at a center.

**Using the center:**
1. A student draws three index cards. He reads the numbers and writes them in the "Lucky Numbers" boxes on his form.
2. He rolls the dice (or cubes) on the mouse pad. He adds the two numbers shown and then records the fact and sum.
3. If the sum matches one of the lucky numbers on his form, he writes "yes." If not, he writes "no."
4. The student repeats the activity until he completes the form.

# Scrabble® Addition

**Skill:** Solving addition facts

**Materials needed:**
- Scrabble® tiles
- a shoebox lid
- several word lists, varying in difficulty
- pencils
- a class supply of paper
- a calculator

**Setting up the center:**
1. Scatter the tiles inside the inverted shoebox lid.
2. Display the materials at a center.

**Using the center:**
1. A student selects a word list.
2. She arranges the tiles to spell the first word.
3. The student uses the numbers at the bottom of the tiles to write an addition sentence. She then adds the numbers to find the value of the word. She records the word, sentence, and sum on a sheet of paper.
4. The student replaces the tiles and repeats the activity for the remaining words.
5. Using the calculator, the student adds the value of all the words to find her total score.

Word List
1. tree
2. park
3. bird
4. swing
5. play

Leslie

tree $1 + 1 + 1 + 1 = 4$
park $3 + 1 + 1 + 5 = 10$
bird $3 + 1 + 1 + 2 = 7$
swing $1 + 4 + 1 + 1 + 2 = 9$
play $3 + 1 + 1 + 4 = 9$

$4 + 10 + 7 + 9 + 9 = 39$

# Let 'em Roll

**Skill:** Solving addition and subtraction facts

**Materials needed:**
- a copy of the gameboard on page 88
- markers
- 18 self-adhesive dots
- 3 dice (or number cubes)
- 2 different game pieces
- a sentence strip numbered 1–18

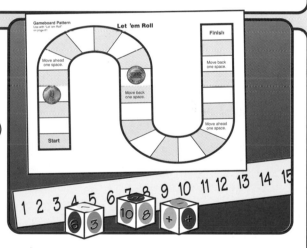

**Setting up the center:**
1. Color the gameboard and laminate it, if desired.
2. Program three dots with addition signs and three dots with subtraction signs.
3. Number six dots 1–6. (Skip if cubes labeled 1–6 are used.)
4. Number six dots 7–12. (Skip if cubes labeled 7–12 are used.)
5. Cover each die or cube with a set of dots. (Do not cover correctly labeled cubes.)

**Using the center:**
1. Two students begin the activity by placing each game piece on Start.
2. Player 1 rolls the dice and answers the addition or subtraction problem made by the numbers and sign rolled.
3. Player 2 checks the answer by counting on the number line.
4. If Player 1 answered correctly, he rolls the die labeled 1–6 and moves forward that many spaces. If he answered incorrectly, he does not move.
5. Player 2 takes a turn. The game continues until a player reaches Finish.

# Fact Challenge

**Skill:** Solving addition (or multiplication) facts

**Materials:**
- a deck of cards
- an addition (or multiplication) chart

**Setting up the center:**
   Display the materials at a center.

**Using the center:**
1. A student arranges a desired number of cards facedown in an array such as the one shown.
2. She flips over two cards and adds (or multiplies) the numbers shown. (Face cards have a value of zero and aces have a value of one.)
3. She checks her answer on the fact chart. If her answer is correct, she keeps the cards. If her answer is incorrect, she flips the cards back over.
4. Play continues until all of the cards are gone.

# Totally Turtle

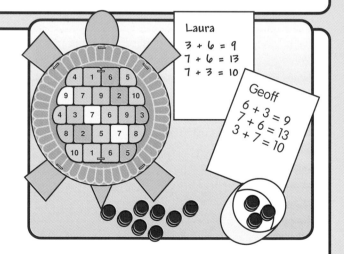

**Skill:** Solving addition (or multiplication) facts

**Materials needed:**
- a cutout of the gameboard pattern on page 89
- a white paper plate
- crayons or markers
- glue
- scissors
- a sheet of green construction paper
- a stapler
- 2 small containers each filled with 12 bingo chips or pennies
- a class supply of paper
- pencils

**Setting up the center:**
1. Color the paper plate and gameboard. Glue the gameboard to the center of the paper plate.
2. Cut four legs, a head, and a tail from green construction paper. Staple the body parts to the paper plate as shown.
3. Display the turtle, containers, paper, and pencils at a center.

**Using the center:**
1. Two students begin the activity by taking one container of chips each.
2. Each player tosses a chip onto the turtle's shell.
3. Each player writes an addition or multiplication fact using the covered numbers.
4. Students compare their answers, then repeat the activity until all of the chips are used.

# Colorful Computation

**Skill:** Solving addition and subtraction word problems

**Materials needed:**
- a supply of M&M's® candies
- a class supply of resealable snack-sized plastic bags
- 10 index cards
- a class supply of paper napkins
- a class supply of paper
- pencils
- a permanent marker

How many red and green M&M's are there in all?

How many more brown M&M's are there than yellow M&M's?

Heather
4 + 6 = 10
7 − 3 = 4

**Setting up the center:**
1. Prepare a snack-sized bag of M&M's® candies for each student. Vary the amount of candies in each bag.
2. Program each index card with a word problem similar to the ones shown.
3. Display the bags, index cards, napkins, paper, pencils, and marker at a center.

**Using the center:**
1. A student empties a bag of M&M's® candies onto a napkin.
2. She chooses an index card and reads the word problem.
3. The student then writes a number sentence for the problem and solves it.
4. After the student solves a predetermined number of word problems, she puts the candy back in the bag. She uses the permanent marker to label the bag with her name and saves the candy for a snacktime treat.

# Card Sharks

**Skill:** Solving addition facts

**Materials needed:**
- 5 cutouts of the shark pattern on page 85
- markers
- glue
- a 12" x 18" sheet of blue construction paper
- a deck of cards with the face cards removed
- pencils
- a class supply of lined paper

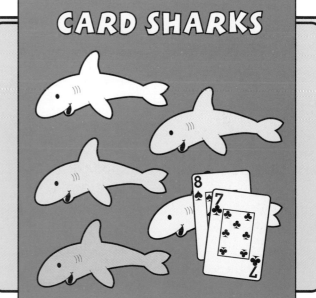

CARD SHARKS

**Setting up the center:**
1. Color each shark cutout. Glue the sharks to the construction paper as shown. Laminate the paper for durability, if desired.
2. Display the shark sheet, cards, pencils, and paper at a center.

**Using the center:**
1. A student places two cards faceup on each shark.
2. He uses the numbers on each pair of cards to write and solve an addition fact on a sheet of paper.
3. To get a total score for the round, the student adds the five sums.
4. If time allows, he puts the cards at the bottom of the deck and repeats the activity for more rounds of play.

# Domino Dots

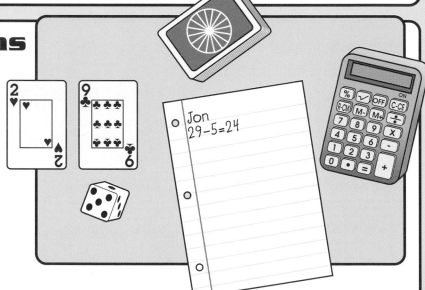

**Skill:** Solving subtraction facts

**Materials needed:**
- a supply of 6" x 12" oaktag strips
- a pencil
- markers
- a supply of self-adhesive dots

**Setting up the center:**
1. Identify a desired number of subtraction facts.
2. Use a pencil to lightly divide each oaktag strip into thirds. Fold the first section over the second section to create a flap.
3. On the outside of the flap, write the minuend from a chosen fact. On the third section, use the self-adhesive dots to make a domino showing the value of the subtrahend. Unfold the strip. Label the first section with the difference and make a domino showing this difference on the second section. Color each section as shown, if desired.
4. Continue in the same manner with each remaining oaktag strip and subtraction fact.
5. Display the domino cards in a center.

**Using the center:**
1. A student chooses a domino card.
2. She determines the hidden number of dots by subtracting the number of dots in view from the number on the folded flap.
3. The student opens the flap to check her answer.
4. She repeats the activity with the remaining domino cards.

# Quick Calculations

**Skill:** Subtracting from two digits

**Materials needed:**
- a deck of cards with the face cards and tens removed
- a class supply of lined paper
- pencils
- a die
- a calculator

**Setting up the center:**
Display the materials at a center.

**Using the center:**
1. A student draws two cards. He uses the cards to make a two-digit number. (Aces have a value of one.) He writes the resulting number on his paper.
2. He rolls the die and subtracts the number shown from the two-digit number.
3. The student uses the calculator to check his work.
4. He repeats the activity a predetermined number of times.

# Cool Facts

**Skill:** Solving basic facts

**Materials needed:**
- a supply of construction paper cutouts of the ice-cream scoop pattern on page 83
- a supply of construction paper cutouts of the ice-cream cone pattern on page 83
- markers
- an empty ice-cream cone box

**Setting up the center:**
1. Program each scoop of ice cream with a different math fact.
2. For each fact, program a cone with the corresponding answer.
3. On the back of each scoop and cone pair, draw a matching symbol.
4. Place the pieces in an empty ice-cream cone box. Display the box at a center.

**Using the center:**
1. A student removes the ice-cream scoops and cones from the box.
2. She reads the math fact on each scoop and places it on the cone with the correct answer.
3. After placing all the cutouts, she turns over each scoop and cone to check her work.

# SPILL THE BEANS

**Skill:** Solving multiplication facts

**Materials needed:**
- red spray paint
- a supply of dried lima beans
- a plastic cup
- a class supply of lined paper
- pencils

**Setting up the center:**
1. Prepare a desired amount of lima beans by painting one side of each bean with red spray paint. Allow them to dry.
2. Place the dried beans in a cup.
3. Display the cup, paper, and pencils at a center.

**Using the center:**
1. A student spills the beans from the cup.
2. He writes the number of red beans visible and the number of unpainted beans visible on his paper; then he multiplies the two numbers together.
3. He returns the beans to the cup and repeats the process ten times, or more if time allows.

# High-Flying Facts

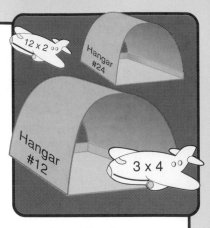

**Skill:** Solving basic facts

**Materials needed:**
- a supply of 9" x 12" sheets of construction paper
- a supply of shoebox lids
- glue
- scissors
- a supply of construction paper cutouts of the airplane pattern on page 90
- markers

**Setting up the center:**
1. To make a hangar, glue the short edges of a sheet of construction paper along the long sides of a shoebox lid to make an arch. Trim away the excess portion of the lid as shown. Repeat this process to make several hangars.
2. Program each side of each hangar with "Hangar # ____." (Fill in the blank with a math fact answer.)
3. Program each airplane cutout with a different math fact whose answer matches a hangar number.
4. Label the bottom of each hangar with the math facts and answers for self-checking.
5. Display the hangars and airplanes at a center.

**Using the center:**
1. A student reads the fact on each airplane and flies it into the hangar with the matching answer.
2. After placing all the planes, she looks at the bottom of the hangar to check her work.

# NESTING FAMILIES

**Skill:** Identifying fact families

**Materials needed:**
- a supply of brown lunch bags
- a supply of blue construction paper cutouts of the bird pattern on page 90
- markers
- scissors

**Setting up the center:**
1. Identify a desired number of different fact families. Program a set of birds with a different math fact in the same family. Repeat this for each fact family.
2. Mark the back of each bird in a set with the same symbol for self-checking.
3. Trim each paper bag to a height of five inches. Roll each bag's edge down to make a nest as shown.
4. Display the birds and the nests at a center.

**Using the center:**
1. A student reads each math fact written on the birds.
2. He arranges each bird with others in the same fact family in a nest.
3. After placing all the birds, the student turns them over to check his work.

# Fact Families at Home

**Skill:** Identifying fact families

**Materials needed:**
- 5 clean ½-pint milk cartons
- a stapler
- a supply of construction paper
- glue
- markers
- 20 clothespins

**Setting up the center:**
1. Staple the top of each milk carton closed.
2. Use construction paper, glue, and markers to decorate the cartons to resemble houses.
3. Program three sides of each house with a different number from a fact family. Label the bottom of each carton with four math facts corresponding to the numbers on the house.
4. Program the clothespins with the same math facts.
5. Display the houses and clothespins at a center.

**Using the center:**
1. A student chooses a clothespin and reads the math fact.
2. She determines to which house the fact belongs and then clips the pin to its roof.
3. After placing all of the pins, she turns over each house to check her work.

# Building a Fact Family House

**Skill:** Identifying fact families

**Materials needed:**
- a class supply of construction paper cutouts of the house pattern on page 91
- 5 brown construction paper cutouts of the hammer pattern on page 91
- markers
- glue
- scissors
- pencils
- a class supply of 8½" x 11" sheets of white paper

**Setting up the center:**
1. Program each hammer with numbers in a fact family.
2. Display the hammers and remaining materials at a center.

**Using the center:**
1. A student chooses a house and then cuts the windows along the dashed lines.
2. He folds the window flaps back along the solid lines. Then he glues the house to a sheet of white paper and trims the excess.
3. The student selects a hammer and then writes the fact family numerals on the roof of his house.
4. He writes a different fact family equation and answer inside each window.

# How Do You Measure Up?

**Skill:** Measuring using standard units

**Materials needed:**
- an assortment of different-colored ribbon
- scissors
- a supply of resealable plastic bags
- rulers
- a class supply of paper
- pencils

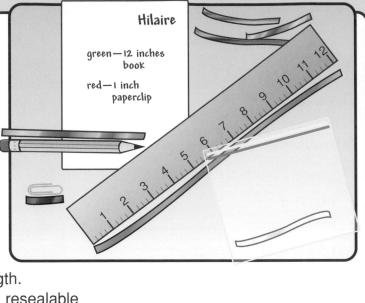

**Setting up the center:**
1. Cut each color of ribbon to a different length.
2. Place one length of each color ribbon in a resealable bag. Prepare several bags for the center.
3. Display the bags, paper, rulers, and pencils at a center.

**Using the center:**
1. A student removes the ribbons from a bag.
2. She uses a ruler to measure each length of ribbon and then records the ribbon color and measurement on her paper.
3. After measuring all the ribbons, she finds a classroom object of the same length as each ribbon and writes its name next to the corresponding measurement.

# Squiggle Estimation

**Skill:** Estimating using nonstandard measurement

**Materials needed:**
- a supply of 9" x 6½" construction paper cards
- markers
- assorted sets of small objects, such as paper clips, Unifix® cubes, and dried beans
- a supply of resealable plastic bags

**Setting up the center:**
1. Use a marker to draw a different squiggly line on each construction paper card.
2. Place each set of objects in a different resealable bag.
3. Display the cards and bags at a center.

**Using the center:**
1. A student selects a squiggle card and a set of objects.
2. He estimates the number of objects needed to cover the line.
3. Then the student places the objects atop the line to determine the actual number needed to cover it.
4. If time allows, he continues the activity using a different card and bag of objects.

# Yarn Art

**Skill:** Measuring using standard units

**Materials needed:**
- a list of 12 different lengths in inches
- a supply of yarn
- a ruler
- scissors
- a class supply of construction paper
- glue

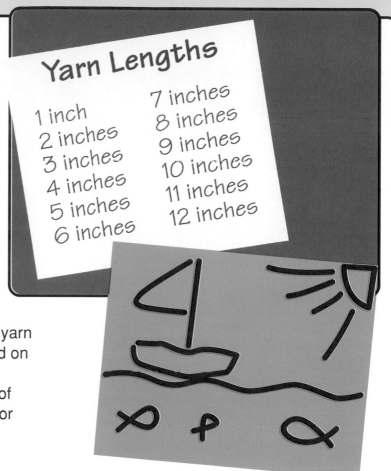

## Yarn Lengths

| | |
|---|---|
| 1 inch | 7 inches |
| 2 inches | 8 inches |
| 3 inches | 9 inches |
| 4 inches | 10 inches |
| 5 inches | 11 inches |
| 6 inches | 12 inches |

**Setting up the center:**
Display the materials at a center.

**Using the center:**
1. A student uses a ruler to measure the yarn and then cuts it in the lengths specified on the posted list.
2. She glues the yarn pieces on a sheet of construction paper to create a picture or design.
3. She places her completed picture in a designated display area.

# Treasure to Measure

**Skill:** Measuring using standard units

**Materials needed:**
- a shoebox with a lid
- a variety of arts-and-crafts supplies
- a variety of costume jewelry pieces
- a measuring tape
- a class supply of paper
- pencils

Beth

4 inches
10 cm

7 inches
18 cm

**Setting up the center:**
1. Decorate the shoebox to resemble a treasure chest.
2. Place the jewelry in the box.
3. Display the treasure chest, measuring tape, paper, and pencils at a center.

**Using the center:**
1. A student selects a piece of jewelry and then draws it on a sheet of paper.
2. He measures the jewelry piece using the measuring tape. He records its measurement, in both inches and centimeters, next to his drawing.
3. The student repeats the activity until he has measured five pieces of jewelry.

# Math Snack

**Skill:** Measuring using standard units

**Materials needed:**
- a recipe card
- a variety of snack food ingredients, such as pretzels, peanuts, cereal, and chocolate chips
- a supply of bowls
- a fine-tipped marker
- a set of measuring cups
- a set of measuring spoons
- a supply of small resealable plastic bags

**Math Snack**

1 serving

Ingredients:

¼ c. pretzels

2 tbsp. peanuts

½ c. cereal

3 tsp. chocolate chips

**Directions:**

Measure each ingredient and then pour it into the bag. Seal the bag; then shake it. Enjoy!

**Setting up the center:**
1. Program a recipe card with the ingredients* and directions for preparing a snack.
2. Place the ingredients in different bowls.
3. Display the recipe card, bowls, resealable bags, and measuring cups and spoons at a center.

\* Be sure to check for student food allergies.

**Using the center:**
1. A student reads the recipe and carefully follows the directions to create her snack mix.
2. Then she puts the prepared snack in a resealable bag for a snacktime treat.

# Time Sentences

**Skill:** Telling time

**Materials needed:**
- a supply of index cards
- a marker
- a class supply of paper
- pencils

Stephen

1. I get home from school at 3:30.

**Setting up the center:**
1. Use a marker to program each index card with a clock face showing a different time.
2. Display the cards, paper, and pencils at a center.

**Using the center:**
1. A student selects a card and then reads the time shown on the face of the clock.
2. He writes a sentence on his paper that includes the time shown on the card.
3. The student continues the activity using different time cards until he has written five time sentences.

# Teatime

**Skill:** Telling time

**Materials needed:**
- 10 construction paper cutouts of the teapot and cup patterns on page 92
- a fine-tipped black marker
- a clock-face stamp
- a stamp pad

**Setting up the center:**
1. Use the marker to write a different time on each teapot.
2. Stamp a clock face on each cup; then program each clock to correspond with a different teapot.
3. Stamp a clock face on the back of each teapot; then program each one for self-checking.
4. Display the teapots and cups at a center.

**Using the center:**
1. A student reads the time on a teapot.
2. She finds the matching cup and places it beside the teapot.
3. She continues in this manner until all matching sets are found.
4. The student turns over the teapots to check her work.

# Time for Poetry

**Skill:** Telling time

**Materials needed:**
- a copy of the clock poem on page 93
- 2 copies of the clock pattern on page 93 for each child
- 13 half sheets of blank paper for each child
- scissors    • markers
- glue    • a stapler

**Setting up the center:**
1. Print a different time in each of the poem's blanks. (Vary the level of difficulty of the times based on students' skill levels.)
2. Display the poem, clock patterns, clock, paper, markers, and stapler at a center.

**Using the center:**
1. A student cuts out each clock and glues it to a half sheet of paper. He reads the poem and takes note of the times mentioned.
2. He records each time on a different clock and then writes and illustrates each verse of the poem.
3. The student compiles his completed pages. He then personalizes and decorates a booklet cover and staples the pages to create a booklet.

# Pocket Watches

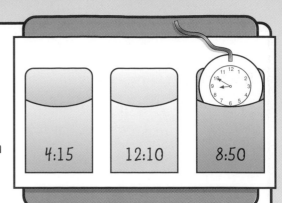

**Skill:** Telling time

**Materials needed:**
- a sheet of poster board
- markers
- a supply of library pockets
- a supply of 2½" construction paper circles, stamped with a clock face
- a supply of 4" lengths of yarn
- clear tape
- a resealable plastic bag

**Setting up the center:**
1. Program each pocket with a different time (see illustration) and then attach the pockets to the poster board with tape. Write the corresponding answers (clock face) on the back of the poster board.
2. Program each construction paper circle with a corresponding time for self-checking. Tape a length of yarn to the back of each one so that it resembles a pocket watch. Store the watches in the bag.
3. Display the poster and bag at a center.

**Using the center:**
1. A student removes the watches from the bag. She chooses a watch and reads the time.
2. She places the watch in the correct pocket.
3. She turns over the poster board to check her work.

# HOW MUCH IS THAT DOGGY IN THE WINDOW?

**Skill:** Adding coins

**Materials needed:**
- 10 animal or seasonal cutouts
- a supply of coin stickers
- a permanent marker
- a class supply of lined paper
- pencils

**Setting up the center:**
1. Put coin stickers in different amounts on each cutout.
2. Number the cutouts; then label the back of each one with the correct sum of money for self-checking. Laminate the cutouts, if desired.
3. Display the cutouts, paper, and pencils at a center.

**Using the center:**
1. A student numbers his paper from 1 to 10.
2. He adds the coin amounts on each cutout; then he writes each total on his paper.
3. After completing the activity, he turns over the cutouts to check his answers.

# Grocery Shopping

**Skill:** Sequencing coin amounts

**Materials needed:**
- a supply of cutout grocery ads
- a supply of 5" x 8" index cards
- glue
- a permanent marker
- a paper or plastic grocery bag
- an assortment of coins

**Setting up the center:**
1. Glue each ad to the blank side of an index card. If desired, label the back of each card with possible coin combinations for self-checking.
2. Place the ads in the bag.
3. Display the bag and coins at a center.

**Using the center:**
1. A student chooses three ads from the grocery bag.
2. She arranges the ads in order from the lowest to the highest price.
3. She places coins in front of each ad to show the correct amount of each item.
4. After completing the cards, she may turn them over to check her work.
5. If time allows, she chooses three more cards from the bag and repeats the activity.

# Coin Calculations

**Skill:** Adding coins

**Materials needed:**
- a sheet of light-colored construction paper
- a permanent marker
- 4 resealable plastic bags
- an assortment of coins
- a sheet of paper (optional)

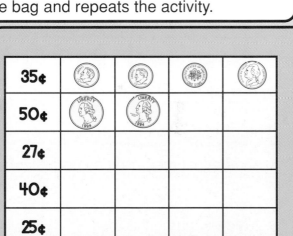

| 35¢ | (dime) | (dime) | (nickel) | (nickel) |
|---|---|---|---|---|
| 50¢ | (quarter) | (quarter) | | |
| 27¢ | | | | |
| 40¢ | | | | |
| 25¢ | | | | |

**Setting up the center:**
1. Using the sheet of construction paper, make a coin calculations chart similar to the one shown. If desired, create an answer key showing all possible coin combinations for each amount on a sheet of paper.
2. Laminate the chart for durability, if desired.
3. Label each resealable bag with a different coin name; then place the coins in the corresponding bags.
4. Display the chart and bags at a center.

**Using the center:**
1. A student looks at the first amount on the chart and places corresponding coins for that amount.
2. He continues in the same manner with the remaining coin amounts.
3. If time allows, he repeats the activity using different combinations of coins. He may check his work using the answer key.

# Sticky Fingers

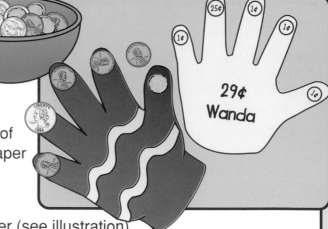

**Skill:** Adding coins

**Materials needed:**
- a glove
- an assortment of plastic coins
- a supply of self-adhesive Velcro® dots
- a plastic bowl
- a class supply of construction paper
- scissors
- pencils

**Setting up the center:**
1. Put a Velcro® dot (hook side) on each glove finger (see illustration).
2. Put a Velcro dot (loop side) on the flat side of each coin; then place the coins in a bowl.
3. Display the glove, bowl, construction paper, scissors, and pencils at a center.

**Using the center:**
1. A student traces her hand on a sheet of construction paper and then cuts out the hand.
2. She puts on the glove, then places her hand in the bowl until at least one coin has stuck to each finger.
3. She removes the coins and then writes the amount of each on the corresponding finger of her hand cutout.
4. She writes the total coin amount in the center of her hand cutout.
5. If time allows, she may repeat the activity, using the other side of the cutout to record her work.

# How Much Do I Owe?

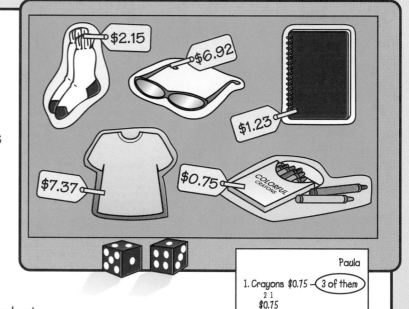

**Skill:** Adding money amounts

**Materials needed:**
- a sheet of poster board
- a variety of magazine cutouts of products
- glue
- markers
- 2 dice or number cubes
- a class supply of paper
- pencils
- calculator

**Setting up the center:**
1. Glue the product cutouts to the poster board.
2. Draw and label a price tag for each product.
3. Display the poster, dice, paper, pencils, and a calculator at a center.

**Using the center:**
1. A student selects a product from the poster.
2. He rolls the dice to determine how many of the product he will purchase.
3. On a sheet of paper he calculates his purchase by adding the prices (or by multiplying the number with the price). He checks his work using a calculator.
4. He continues the activity, selecting and purchasing a predetermined number of products.

# Corner Grocery

**Skill:** Adding money

**Materials needed:**
- a supply of self-adhesive labels
- a permanent marker
- an assortment of clean, empty food packages
- several old wallets
- an assortment of paper money and coins
- a sheet of paper (optional)

**Setting up the center:**
1. Program a different price on each adhesive label; then attach each one to a different food package.
2. Label each wallet with a letter; then put a different amount of paper money and coins in each.
3. If desired, program a sheet of paper with all possible food purchases for each wallet amount.
4. Display the wallets and food packages at a center.

**Using the center:**
1. A student selects a wallet, removes the money, and then counts it.
2. She chooses two food items that she would be able to purchase using the given money amount. She may check her work using the answer key.
3. If time allows, she may choose another wallet and repeat the activity.

# Special Delivery

**Skill:** Calculating area

**Materials needed:**
- construction paper cutouts of the package patterns on page 94
- a shoebox
- a variety of arts-and-crafts supplies
- markers
- 20 one-inch construction paper squares
- a class supply of lined paper
- pencils

**Setting up the center:**
1. Decorate the shoebox to resemble a mail truck; then put the package cutouts and paper squares inside it.
2. Program the truck bottom with the correct answers for self-checking.
3. Display the truck, lined paper, and pencils at a center.

**Using the center:**
1. A student numbers a sheet of paper from 1 to 8.
2. He chooses a package from the truck and then determines the area by placing paper squares on top of the package shape.
3. He counts the squares, then records his answer on the paper.
4. After the truck is empty, he turns it over to check his work.

# GEOMETRIC PICTURES

**Skill:** Identifying geometric shapes

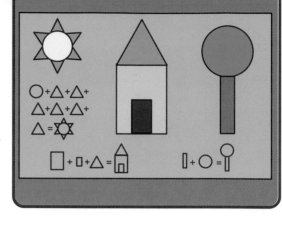

**Materials needed:**
- an assortment of construction paper shapes
- a resealable plastic bag
- a class supply of 12" x 18" sheets of construction paper
- glue
- pencils

**Setting up the center:**
1. Store the construction paper shapes in the bag.
2. Display the bag, construction paper, glue, and pencils at a center.

**Using the center:**
1. A student chooses a variety of different shapes. She glues the shapes to a sheet of construction paper to create a picture.
2. She writes a shape equation for each item in her picture (see illustration).
3. She places her picture in a designated display area.

# Geometric Grab Bag

**Skill:** Identifying geometric shapes

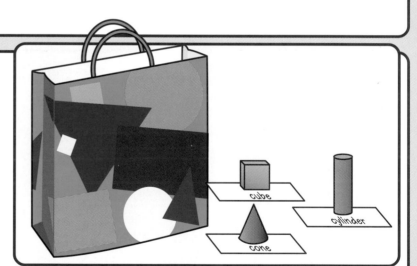

**Materials needed:**
- a supply of index cards
- markers
- an assortment of geometric shapes
- a large gift bag

**Setting up the center:**
1. Program each index card with the name of each of the geometric shapes. Include the number of corners, faces, and sides on each card, if desired.
2. Place the geometric shapes in the bag.
3. Display the bag and cards at a center.

**Using the center:**
1. A student chooses a card and then reads the shape name.
2. He reaches into the bag and feels for a matching shape.
3. He places the shape on top of the index card.
4. The child repeats the activity until the bag is empty.

# Shapely and Delicious

**Skill:** Identifying shapes

**Materials needed:**
- crackers and cereal in a variety of geometric shapes
- a bowl for each shape
- glue
- a class supply of 6" x 9" white construction paper sheets
- markers or crayons
- a hole puncher
- a length of yarn
- a teacher-designed cover

**Setting up the center:**
1. Place the crackers and cereal in bowls.
2. Display the filled bowls and remaining materials at a center.

**Using the center:**
1. A student chooses a shape. She determines a picture she can create using the shape (see the example shown).
2. She glues the shape (or more than one shape) to a sheet of construction paper. She uses markers or crayons to draw her picture around the shape(s).
3. After each student completes her page, hole-punch the pages at the top, place the decorative cover atop the compiled pages, and tie the pages together with yarn.

# Grab-Bag Graphs

**Skill:** Graphing

**Materials needed:**
- 5 of each color of counting block: red, yellow, green, and blue
- a gift bag
- 1 of each color of crayon: red, yellow, green, and blue
- a class supply of the "Grab Bag Graphs" form on page 95
- pencils

**Setting up the center:**
1. Place the counting blocks inside the bag.
2. Display the bag, crayons, forms, and pencils at a center.

**Using the center:**
1. A student reaches into the bag and removes a counting block. He colors a square on his graphing form to match the block.
2. He repeats Step 1 nine times.
3. He completes the graph as directed on the form.

# Pattern Parade

**Skill:** Identifying patterns

**Materials needed:**
- a 9" x 12" tagboard sheet
- a variety of stickers
- scissors
- a sheet of paper
- a large resealable plastic bag

**Setting up the center:**
1. Cut the tagboard into six two-inch strips.
2. On each strip, adhere stickers in a specific pattern. If desired, laminate the strips for durability.
3. On a separate sheet of paper, create an answer key for each pattern strip.
4. Cut off the last sticker from each strip.
5. Store the strips and pieces in the bag. Display the bag at a center.

**Using the center:**
1. A student removes the strips from the bag.
2. She lays out each strip and determines which piece will complete the patterns.
3. She uses the answer key to check her work.

# Tasty Patterns

**Skill:** Identifying patterns

**Materials needed:**
- a variety of snack foods, such as Cheerios® cereal, marshmallows, chocolate chips, Gummy bears, crackers, M&M's® candies, and pretzels
- glue
- a supply of construction paper
- a bowl for each kind of food

**Setting up the center:**
1. Create a sample pattern like the one shown and glue it to a sheet of construction paper.
2. Place each snack food in a separate bowl.
3. Display the bowls of food, the construction paper, glue, and sample pattern at a center.

**Using the center:**
1. A student chooses three to four different types and amounts of snack foods. He determines a pattern he can create using the foods. He glues the patterned food to a sheet of construction paper.
2. Using the same type and number of foods, he creates a different pattern and glues it to the sheet of paper.
3. He places his patterns in a designated display area.

# Stamp Story Problems

**Skill:** Solving story problems

**Materials needed:**
- a variety of seasonal stamps
- an ink pad
- a supply of lined paper
- a folder
- pencils

While walking home from school, two bats followed me to my house. Then I saw four pumpkins sitting on my porch. How many things did I see in all?

4 pumpkins + 2 bats = 6 in all

pumpkin

bat

**Setting up the center:**
1. Make a sample story problem following the directions below.
2. Display the materials and the sample at a center.

**Using the center:**
1. A student selects two stamps and makes a set of each stamp on a sheet of paper.
2. She writes a story problem that corresponds with the type and number of stamps.
3. On the back of her paper, she writes the number sentence with its answer to show how the problem is solved.
4. She places her completed paper in the folder.
5. If time allows the student selects a different story problem from the folder and solves it on another sheet of paper.

# Fact Finders

**Skill:** Solving problems

**Materials needed:**
- 20 counters
- 10 index cards, numbered from 1 to 10
- a marker
- a class supply of paper
- pencils

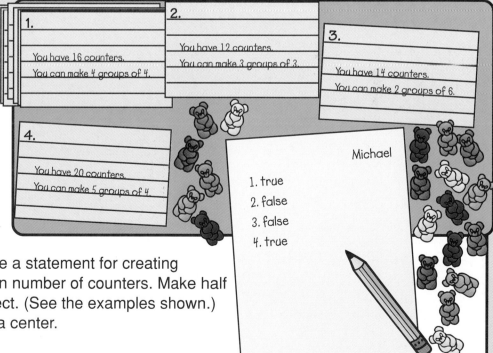

1. You have 16 counters. You can make 4 groups of 4.

2. You have 12 counters. You can make 3 groups of 3.

3. You have 14 counters. You can make 2 groups of 6.

4. You have 20 counters. You can make 5 groups of 4.

Michael
1. true
2. false
3. false
4. true

**Setting up the center:**
1. On each index card, write a statement for creating equal groups with a given number of counters. Make half of the statements incorrect. (See the examples shown.)
2. Display the materials at a center.

**Using the center:**
1. A student numbers a sheet of paper from 1 to 10.
2. He selects a card and tries to group the counters according to the statement.
3. He must use all of the counters described on the index card.
4. After determining if the statement is true or false, he writes "true" or "false" by the corresponding number on his paper.

# Shopping Spree

**Skill:** Solving problems

**Materials needed:**
- sale ads, book order forms, menus, or toy catalogs
- pencils
- a class supply of lined paper
- a calculator

**Setting up the center:**
Display the materials at a center.

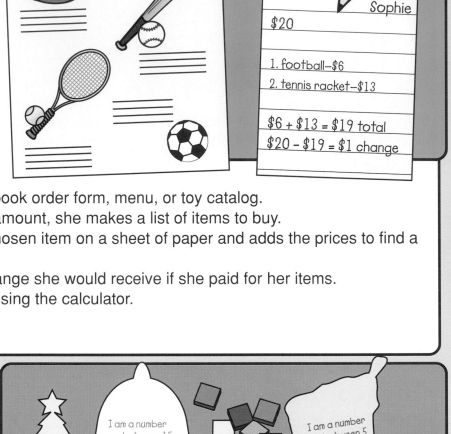

**Using the center:**
1. A student chooses a sale ad, book order form, menu, or toy catalog.
2. Using a predetermined dollar amount, she makes a list of items to buy.
3. She writes the price of each chosen item on a sheet of paper and adds the prices to find a total.
4. She determines how much change she would receive if she paid for her items.
5. The student checks her work using the calculator.

# Digit Detective

**Skill:** Solving problems

**Materials needed:**
- a supply of counting blocks
- a hundreds chart
- a supply of index cards or seasonal cutouts
- markers

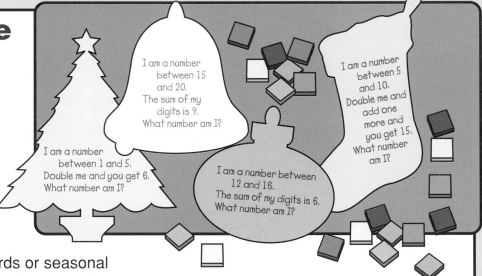

**Setting up the center:**
1. Program a set of index cards or seasonal cutouts with clues similar to the ones shown.
2. Write the correct answer on the back of each card for self-checking.
3. Display the clue cards, counting blocks, and hundreds chart at a center.

**Using the center:**
1. A student picks a card and reads the clues.
2. He uses the clues to determine the number being described. If needed, he uses the counting blocks and the hundreds chart to help find the answer.
3. After determining the answer, he turns over the card to check his work.
4. If time allows, the student selects another clue card to solve.

# Penguin Food

**Skill:** Graphing

**Materials needed:**
- a supply of Goldfish® tiny crackers in three different flavors
- a supply of snack-sized resealable plastic bags
- a supply of the graphing form on page 96
- pencils
- markers or crayons

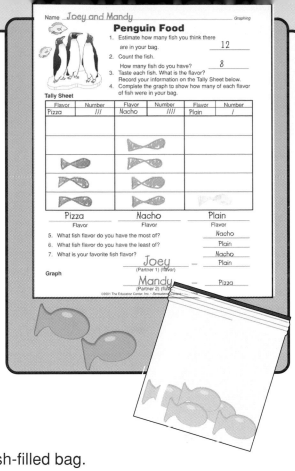

**Setting up the center:**
1. Put the different-flavored fish crackers in each snack-sized bag (no more than five of each flavor).
2. Display the filled bags, forms, and remaining and pencils at a center.

**Using the center:**
1. Students work in pairs, with each pair taking one fish-filled bag.
2. Using its selected bag of fish, each pair completes the graphing sheet as directed on that page.

# Scrabble® Graph

**Skill:** Organizing data, graphing

**Materials needed:**
- a supply of Scrabble® tiles or numbered letter squares made from construction paper
- a small container
- a class supply of blank paper
- markers or crayons

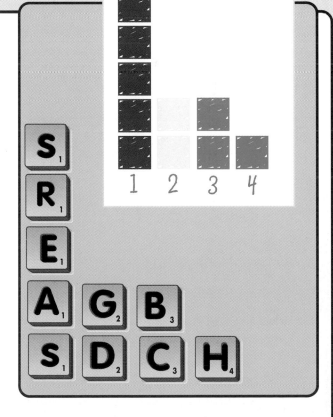

**Setting up the center:**
1. Place the tiles in the container.
2. Display the container, paper, and pencils at a center.

**Using the center:**
1. A student chooses ten tiles.
2. He sorts the tiles according to the values on each one.
3. He draws the results of his sorting on a sheet of paper (see the example shown).

# Words for Sale

**Skill:** Using a calculator

**Materials needed:**
- a supply of plain index cards
- markers
- an envelope
- a chart with prices for each letter of the alphabet (see the example)
- a class supply of blank paper
- pencils
- a calculator

**Setting up the center:**
1. Program each index card with a word like *cat, zoo,* or *math.*
2. Store the index cards in the envelope.
3. Display the envelope and remaining materials at a center.

**Using the center:**
1. A student creates a chart on her paper like the one shown. She selects a word card from the envelope and writes the word on her chart.
2. Using the price chart, she records the prices of the letters in each word.
3. She uses the calculator to add together the total price of each word and records it on the paper.
4. If time allows, the student selects another word card to price.

| A = $1.00 | O = $15.00 |
| B = $2.00 | P =$16.00 |
| C = $3.00 | Q =$17.00 |
| D = $4.00 | R =$18.00 |
| E = $5.00 | S =$19.00 |
| F= $6.00 | T =$20.00 |
| G = $7.00 | U =$21.00 |
| H = $8.00 | V =$22.00 |
| I = $9.00 | W =$23.00 |
| J = $10.00 | X =$24.00 |
| K =$11.00 | Y =$25.00 |
| L =$12.00 | Z =$26.00 |
| M =$13.00 | |
| N = $14.00 | |

**Hannah**

| Words | Letter $ | Total |
| --- | --- | --- |
| CAT | 3+1+20 | $24.00 |
| ZOO | 26+15+15 | $56.00 |

ZOO

---

# Aging Inventions

**Skill:** Using a calculator

**Materials needed:**
- a list of inventions with the years in which they were invented
- a calculator
- a class supply of lined paper
- pencils

**Setting up the center:**
Display the materials at a center.

**Using the center:**
1. A student chooses 8 to 10 inventions.
2. He uses the calculator to determine how old each invention is.
3. He records the information on a sheet of paper.

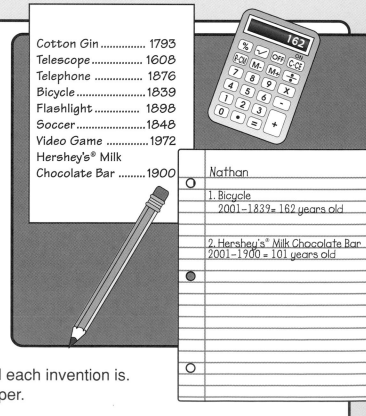

Cotton Gin .............. 1793
Telescope ................ 1608
Telephone .............. 1876
Bicycle ...................... 1839
Flashlight .............. 1898
Soccer ...................... 1848
Video Game ............. 1972
Hershey's® Milk
Chocolate Bar ......... 1900

Nathan
1. Bicycle
   2001–1839= 162 years old

2. Hershey's® Milk Chocolate Bar
   2001–1900 = 101 years old

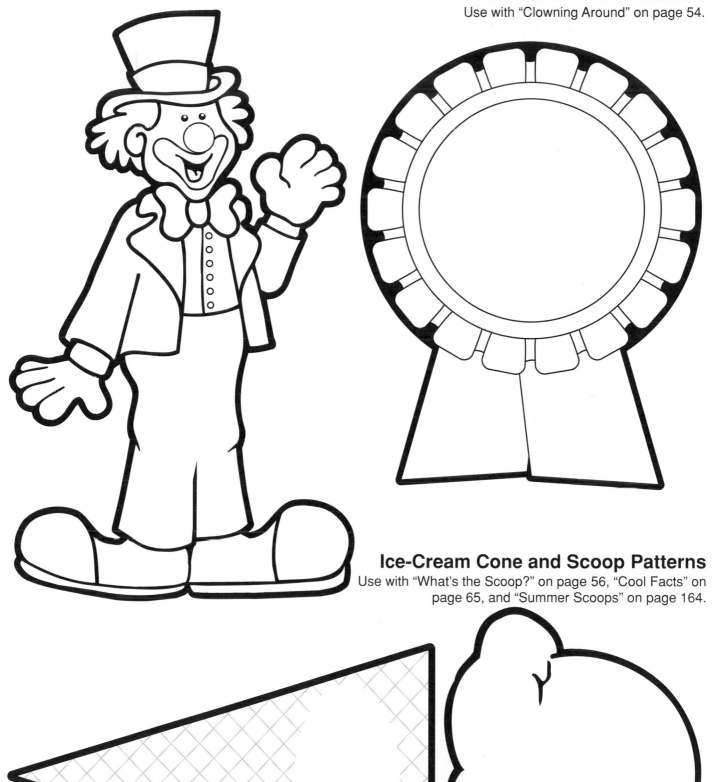

## Ice-Cream Cone and Scoop Patterns
Use with "What's the Scoop?" on page 56, "Cool Facts" on page 65, and "Summer Scoops" on page 164.

# Crayon Box and Crayon Patterns
Use with "A Few Odd Crayons" on page 55.

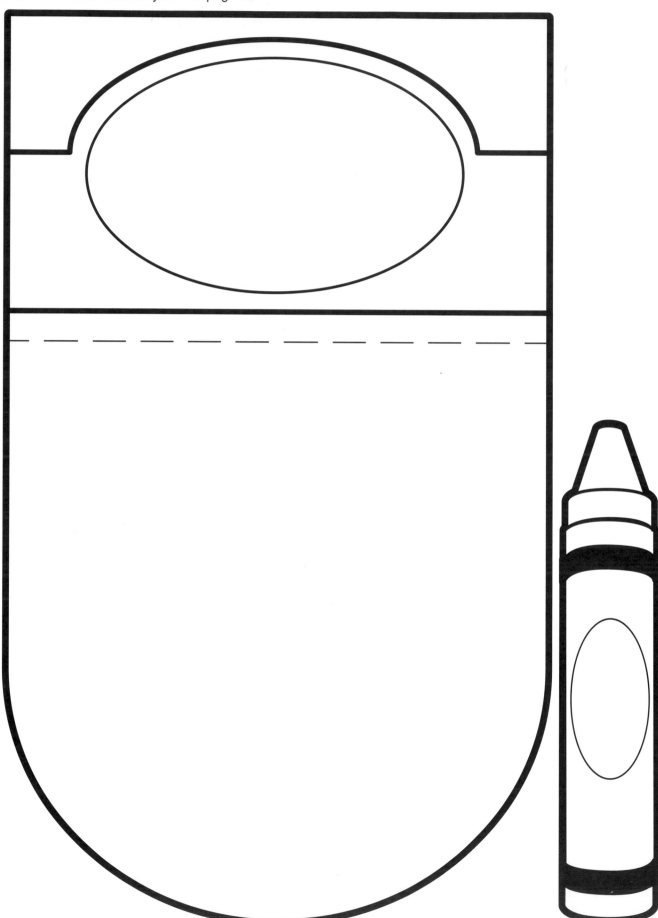

## Cards Form

Use with "High, Low, Three in a Row" on page 57.

### High, Low, Three in a Row

| Low | High | My 3 cards |
|-----|------|------------|
| | | |
| | | |
| | | |
| | | |
| | | |

©2001 The Education Center, Inc.

Name _____

## Shark Pattern

Use with "Card Sharks" on page 63.

# Pizza Slice Pattern

Use with "Pizza...Count Me In!" on page 59.

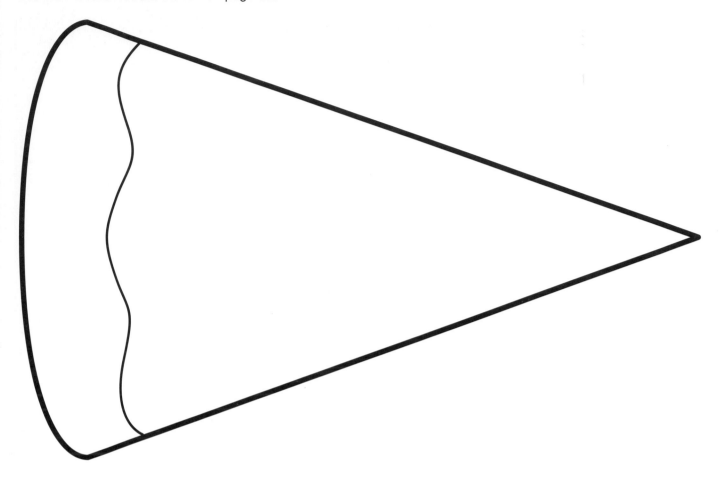

# Gumball Machine Pattern

Use with "Gumball Math" on page 59.

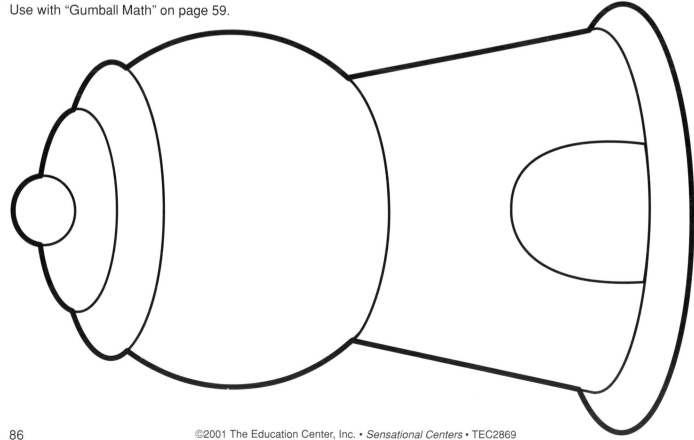

Name _____

# Lucky Numbers

Lucky Numbers: ☐ ☐ ☐

| Fact | Sum | Lucky Number? yes or no |
|------|-----|-------------------------|
| ☐ + ☐ = | _____ | |
| ☐ + ☐ = | _____ | |
| ☐ + ☐ = | _____ | |
| ☐ + ☐ = | _____ | |
| ☐ + ☐ = | _____ | |
| ☐ + ☐ = | _____ | |
| ☐ + ☐ = | _____ | |
| ☐ + ☐ = | _____ | |
| ☐ + ☐ = | _____ | |

**Note to the teacher:** Use with "Lucky Numbers" on page 60.

## Gameboard Pattern
Use with "Let 'em Roll"
on page 61.

## Let 'em Roll

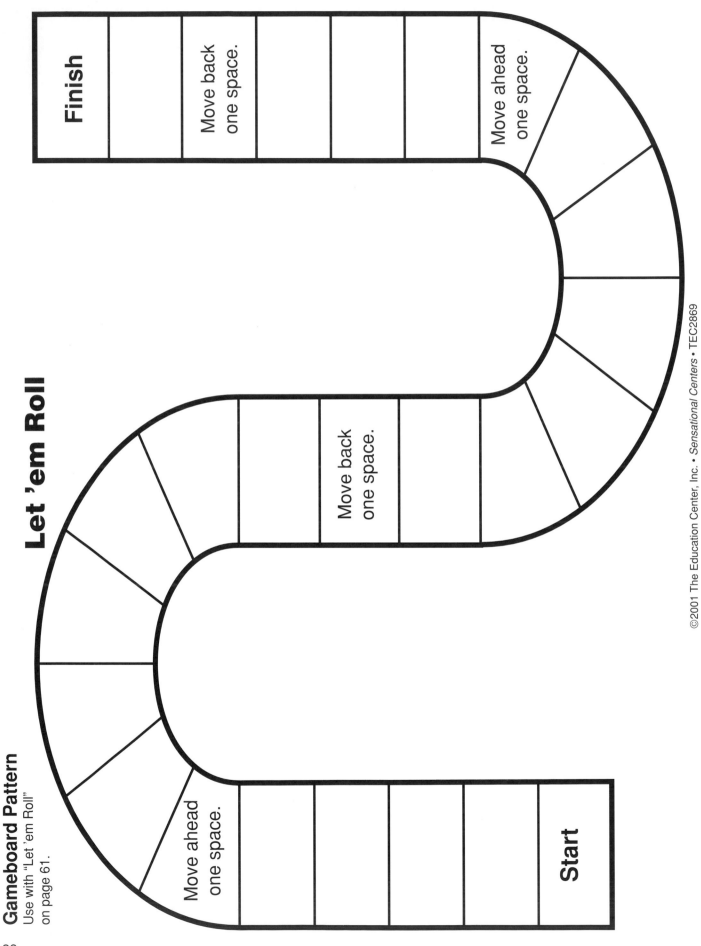

**Finish**

Move back
one space.

Move ahead
one space.

Move back
one space.

Move ahead
one space.

**Start**

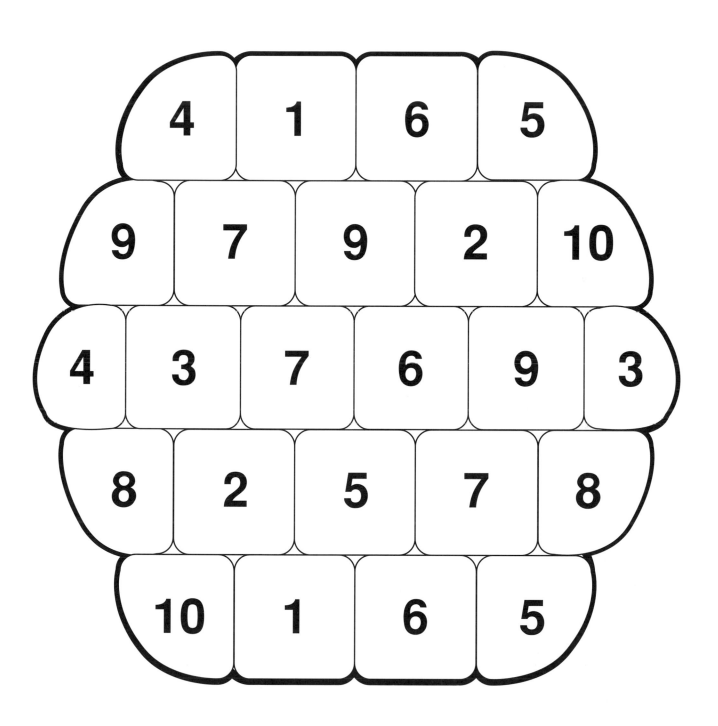

## Airplane Pattern
Use with "High-Flying Facts" on page 66.

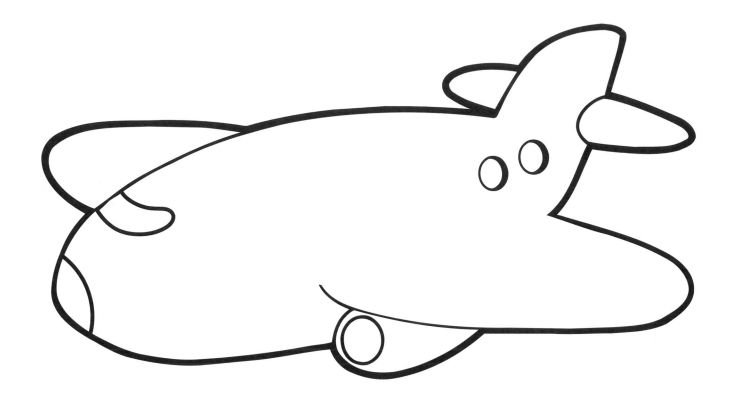

## Bird Pattern
Use with "Nesting Families" on page 66.

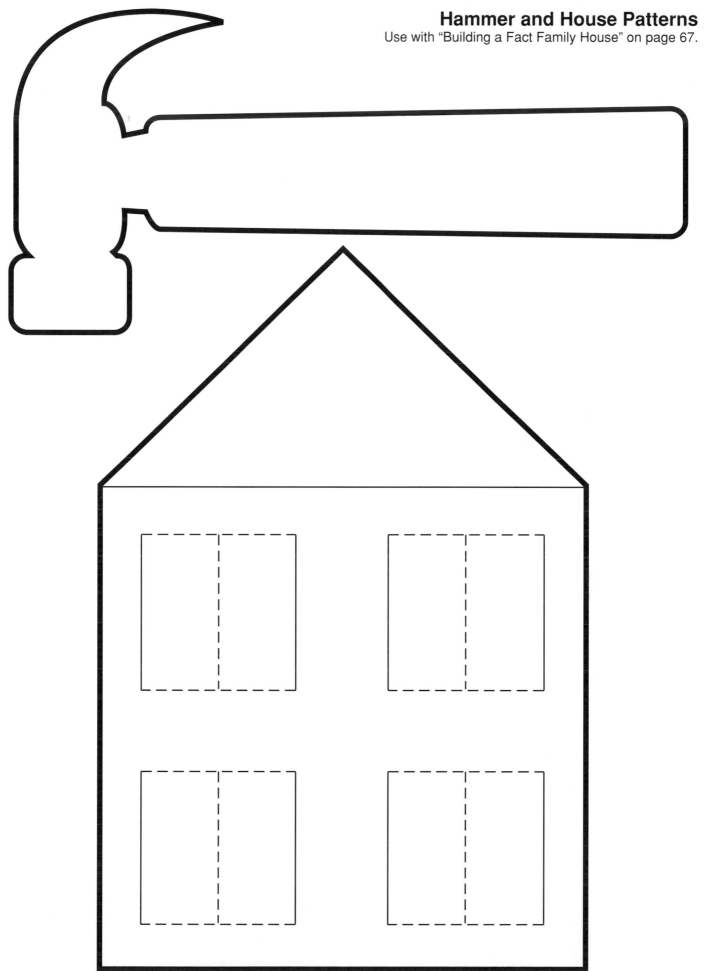

# Teapot and Cup Patterns
Use with "Teatime" on page 71.

There once was a lady
Who lived with her cat.
She ate all the time,
Some of this, some of that.

All day long she would eat, eat, eat;
More than three meals—oh, what a treat!
She snacked from morning till bedtime at night;
Her poor skinny cat never got one bite.

At _____ she ate nine scrambled eggs.
At _____ she gobbled up two chicken legs.

At _____ she munched on three apple pies.
At _____ she enjoyed tons of french fries.

At _____ she chomped on potato chips.
At _____ she licked the last of the dip.

At _____ she grabbed all the cookies from the jar.
At _____ she had a giant candy bar.

At _____ she nibbled ten slices of cheese.
At _____ she buttered up four bowls of peas.

At _____ she felt quite overfed.
At _____ she went to bed.

Oh....

So....

Sick!

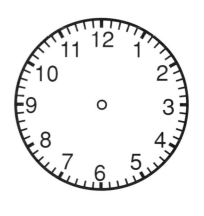

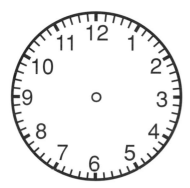

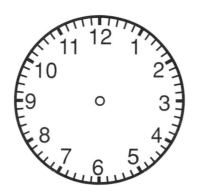

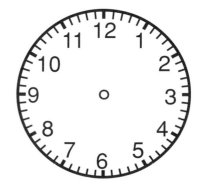

# Package Patterns
Use with "Special Delivery" on page 75.

©2001 The Education Center, Inc. • *Sensational Centers* • TEC2869

Name _____

# Grab-Bag Graphs

 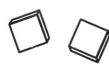  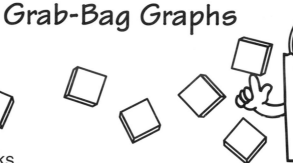 

Show the colors of the blocks.

| 1 | 2 | 3 | 4 | 5 | 6 | 7 | 8 | 9 | 10 |

Make a graph to show the colors.

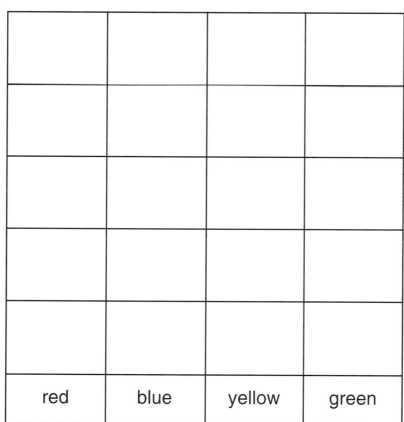

| | | | |
|---|---|---|---|
| | | | |
| | | | |
| | | | |
| | | | |
| red | blue | yellow | green |

Write four sentences about your graph.

1. _____

2. _____

3. _____

4. _____

**Note to the teacher:** Use with "Grab-Bag Graphs" on page 77.

*Graphing*

# Penguin Food

1. Estimate how many fish you think there are in your bag. _____
2. Count the fish. How many do you have? _____
3. Taste each fish. What is the flavor? How many of each flavor do you have? Record your information on the tally sheet below.
4. Complete the graph to show how many of each flavor of fish were in your bag.

## Tally Sheet

| Flavor | Number | Flavor | Number | Flavor | Number |
|--------|--------|--------|--------|--------|--------|
|        |        |        |        |        |        |

## Graph

| | | |
|---|---|---|
| | | |
| | | |
| | | |
| | | |
| | | |

| Flavor | Flavor | Flavor |
|--------|--------|--------|

5. What fish flavor do you have the most of? _____
6. What fish flavor do you have the least of? _____
7. What is your favorite fish flavor?

| _____ | — | _____ |
|:---:|:---:|:---:|
| (Partner 1) | | (flavor) |
| _____ | — | _____ |
| (Partner 2) | | (flavor) |

# Science

# Living or Not?

**Skill:** Identifying living and nonliving things

**Materials needed:**
- eight 3" x 5" index cards, cut in half
- 15 small pictures of living and nonliving things
- glue
- a 12" x 18" sheet of construction paper
- transparent tape
- a marker
- 15 construction paper strips

**Setting up the center:**
1. Glue one picture to each card (discard the one remaining card). Arrange the cards on the construction paper, taping the top edges to the paper as shown.
2. Flip each card, labeling the space beneath it "living" or "nonliving" as appropriate.
3. Program a corresponding number of paper strips "living" or "nonliving."
4. Display the resulting construction paper and paper strips at a center.

**Using the center:**
1. A student looks at a picture and decides if the item shown is living or nonliving.
2. She places the correct strip below the picture.
3. After placing all of the strips, the student lifts each card to check her work.

# LIFE QUESTIONS

**Skill:** Identifying living and nonliving things

**Materials needed:**
- a 9" x 12" sheet of construction paper
- a marker
- 2 shoeboxes with lids
- 2 duplicate sets of pictures showing living and natural nonliving things
- glue

Life Questions
Does it need food?
Does it need water?
Does it need air?

**Setting up the center:**
1. Copy the life questions shown on a sheet of construction paper.
2. Label one shoebox "Living" and the other "Nonliving."
3. Sort one set of pictures into the corresponding box lids. Glue the pictures in place.
4. Place each box inside its matching inverted lid as shown.
5. Display the remaining set of pictures, boxes, and life questions at a center.

**Using the center:**
1. A student chooses a picture. He uses the life questions to help him decide if the item shown is living or nonliving. He places the picture in the appropriate box.
2. He continues in the same manner with the remaining pictures.
3. After placing all the pictures, he lifts each box to check his work.

# Living Matters

**Skill:** Classifying living and nonliving things

**Materials needed:**
- 8 pictures each of living things (plants or animals), the items produced from those living things, and other nonliving items
- 24 index cards
- glue
- 2 sentence strips, labeled "Living" and "Nonliving"

**Setting up the center:**
1. Glue each picture to an index card.
2. Pair the pictures of living items with the items produced from them. Program the back of each pair of cards with a number from 1 to 8 for self-checking.
3. Program the back of each remaining card (nonliving items) with "no match."
4. Laminate the cards, if desired.
5. Display the cards and sentence strips at a center.

**Using the center:**
1. The student chooses a card. She decides if the item pictured is living or nonliving and then places it under the correct sentence strip.
2. If she chooses a card that is part of a pair, she places the card beside its match as shown. (For example, a "living" chicken would be paired with a "nonliving" drumstick.)
3. After placing the cards, she flips over each one to check her work.

# Container Classifications

**Skill:** Classifying animals

**Materials needed:**
- 6 medium-sized containers
- a permanent marker
- 6 blank index cards
- a supply of animal pictures, drawn or cut from magazines
- tape

**Setting up the center:**
1. Label each container with a different animal category as shown.
2. At the top of each index card, list a different animal category and the corresponding animals shown in the pictures. Tape each list to the bottom of its matching container.
3. Display the containers and pictures at a center.

**Using the center:**
1. A students chooses a picture and determines the correct animal category. He places the card in that container.
2. He repeats the activity for the remaining cards.
3. After placing all the cards, he checks his work by referring to the list on the bottom of each container.

# Animal Blocks

**Skill:** Researching animals

**Materials needed:**
- a class supply of the cube pattern on page 120
- a variety of nonfiction animal books
- pencils
- crayons or colored pencils
- scissors
- transparent tape

**Setting up the center:**
 Display the materials at a center.

**Using the center:**
1. The student chooses an animal to research.
2. She gathers a fact related to each category shown on the cube by reading the books provided.
3. The student writes each animal fact in the appropriate space on the cube and then draws a picture of the animal.
4. To make the cube, the student cuts out the pattern, folds it along the dashed lines, and tapes it along the tabs.

# Build a Bug

**Skill:** Identifying insect body parts

**Materials needed:**
- craft materials to represent the parts of an insect (for example, *body parts*—Styrofoam® pieces, large pom-poms; *legs*—yarn, pipe cleaners; *antennae*—wire bits, straws; *eyes*—small pom-poms, beads; *wings*—lace, cellophane)
- 5 containers, labeled as shown
- a class supply of the "Build-a-Bug Checklist" on page 121
- a class supply of 9" x 12" sheets of light-colored construction paper
- glue     • scissors     • pencils

**Setting up the center:**
1. Sort the craft materials into the labeled containers.
2. Display the containers, checklists, construction paper, glue, scissors, and pencils at a center.

**Using the center:**
1. A student chooses an insect. He then chooses the appropriate number of materials to represent each part of his insect's body.
2. He creates his insect by gluing the materials onto the construction paper.
3. The student uses a pencil to label his insect's body parts.
4. He completes the checklist to make sure that his insect has all of its body parts.

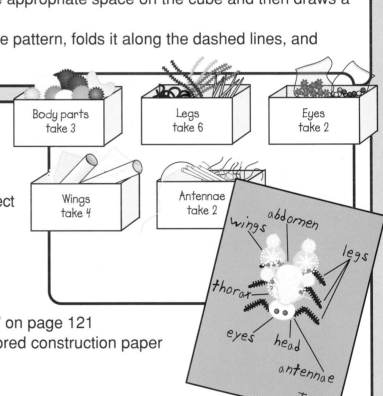

# Is It a Helper? Is It a Pest?

**Skill:** Classifying insects

**Materials needed:**
- a 9" x 12" sheet of construction paper
- a sheet of paper    • scissors
- markers    • glue
- a copy of the insect cards on page 122
- a copy of the insect information card on page 122
- a 5" x 7" construction paper rectangle

**Setting up the center:**
1. Draw a Venn diagram on the construction paper. Label the diagram "Helper," "Both," and "Pest" as shown. On a sheet of paper, draw a second Venn diagram labeled with correct answers as shown.
2. Cut out the insect cards and the insect information card. Glue the information card to the construction paper rectangle.
3. Display the Venn diagram, insect cards, insect information card, and answer key at a center.

**Using the center:**
1. A student reads the information card.
2. In turn, she places each insect card in the appropriate section of the Venn diagram.
3. After placing all the cards, she uses the answer key to check her work.

---

# Thumbprint Life Cycles

**Skill:** Understanding the life cycle of a butterfly

**Materials needed:**
- a class supply of paper plates
- markers
- a dark-colored stamp pad

**Setting up the center:**
1. Use a marker to divide a paper plate into four equal sections as shown.
2. Make a sample detailing the life cycle of a butter-fly on the paper plate as shown.
3. Add decorative details as desired.
4. Display the sample and materials at a center.

**Using the center:**
1. A student sections a paper plate and stamps his thumbprint in each resulting section as shown on the sample.
2. He labels each section of the sample with the appropriate life-cycle stage. He then completes a drawing illustrating each stage.

# Dinosaur Dinners

**Skill:** Classifying dinosaurs

**Materials needed:**
- books featuring dinosaurs
- a class supply of small paper plates
- crayons
- transparent tape
- a class supply of safety pins

**Setting up the center:**
Display the materials at a center.

**Using the center:**
1. A student selects a dinosaur from one of the books.
2. She draws her chosen dinosaur on a paper plate.
3. She draws a green border around the plate if her dinosaur was a plant eater and a brown border around the plate if her dinosaur was a meat eater.
4. She tapes a safety pin to the back of her plate to create a button.
5. She displays her button in a designated area. After all students have visited the center, invite them to share their buttons.

# Fragrant Pictures

**Skill:** Recognizing parts of a flower

**Materials needed:**
- a supply of live flowers
- a chart identifying the parts of a flower
- a class supply of 9" x 12" sheets of white construction paper

**Setting up the center:**
Display the materials at a center.

**Using the center:**
1. A student selects several flowers. He refers to the chart to locate the petals and then carefully removes them from each flower.
2. He firmly presses each petal against a sheet of construction paper, smudging each one to create a colorful picture.
3. He posts his picture in a designated display area.

# Foliage Fun

**Skill:** Classifying leaves

**Materials needed:**
- a class supply of the foliage form on page 123
- a supply of leaves with varying edges and vein patterns
- crayons with the wrappers removed

**Setting up the center:**
Display the materials at a center.

**Using the center:**
1. A student studies the leaf patterns shown on page 123. She chooses a pattern and then finds a leaf that matches it.
2. She places the leaf underneath the paper on the appropriate section of her form. (See the example shown.) She then rubs the side of a crayon on the paper above the leaf to create an imprint, or rubbing, of it.
3. She repeats Steps 1–2 for each leaf pattern on her form.

# Getting the Scoop on Soil

**Skill:** Examining a soil sample

**Materials needed:**
- a container of garden soil filled with objects such as small twigs, parts of leaves, pebbles, etc.
- a laundry detergent scoop
- a shallow pan
- a class supply of blank paper
- pencils
- craft sticks

**Setting up the center:**
Display the materials at a center.

**Using the center:**
1. A student pours a scoopful of soil into a shallow pan.
2. With a craft stick, he examines the soil and separates the objects he finds from the rest of the sample.
3. He draws and labels each object he finds on a sheet of paper.

# Serving Up Nutrition

**Skill:** Understanding healthy eating habits

**Materials needed:**
- 3 paper plates
- markers
- a variety of plastic foods representative of the basic food groups

**Setting up the center:**
1. Program the fronts of each of three paper plates with different requirements for a healthy breakfast, lunch, and dinner as shown in the example.
2. Display the paper plates and plastic foods at a center.

**Using the center:**
1. A student selects a plate and reads the healthy meal requirements.
2. She chooses one food to match each serving description and places it on the plate.
3. If time allows, she may prepare another meal.

Lunch
Bread group: 1 serving
Meat group: 1 serving
Fruit and vegetable group:
2 servings
Dairy group: 1 serving

# Planet Puzzles

**Skill:** Studying planets

**Materials needed:**
- nine 6" construction paper circles
- scissors
- markers
- a picture book about the solar system
- a large resealable plastic bag

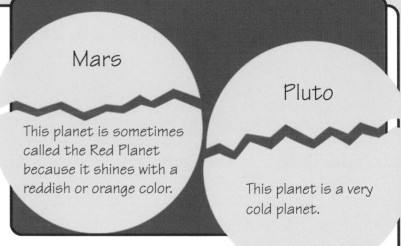

Mars

This planet is sometimes called the Red Planet because it shines with a reddish or orange color.

Pluto

This planet is a very cold planet.

**Setting up the center:**
1. Make a zigzag cut down the center of one circle.
2. Program one piece of the circle with the name of a planet.
3. Read the book to find one fact about the planet. Program the other piece of the circle with the fact.
4. Make a different zigzag cut down the center of each remaining circle. Then repeat Steps 2–3 for each remaining planet.
5. Store the planet pieces in a resealable plastic bag. Display the bag and book at a center.

**Using the center:**
1. A student removes the planet pieces from the bag and arranges them on a table or workspace.
2. He reads the book and then matches each planet name to the correct planet fact.

# Star Bright

**Skill:** Making a constellation

**Materials needed:**
- a class supply of 4½" x 6" pieces of black construction paper
- a book of constellation illustrations
- white crayons
- sharpened pencils
- transparent tape

**Setting up the center:**
Display the materials at a center.

**Using the center:**
1. A student chooses a constellation from the book.
2. She uses a crayon to make dots on her paper to represent the stars in the pattern of the constellation.
3. She uses a pencil to punch holes in the paper where the dots have been drawn.
4. She writes the name of the constellation on her paper with the crayon.
5. After completing the project, she tapes it to a window.

# Partly Cloudy, Partly Cotton

**Skill:** Identifying cloud types

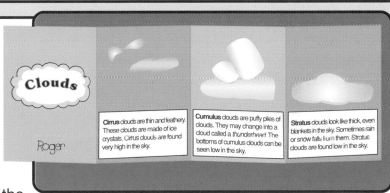

**Materials needed:**
- a class supply of 6" x 18" blue construction paper strips
- a class supply of the booklet patterns at the bottom of page 121
- a supply of cotton balls
- scissors
- glue
- reference books identifying the different cloud types

**Setting up the center:**
1. Accordion-fold each blue construction paper strip into four equal parts.
2. Display the strips and remaining materials at a center.

**Using the center:**
1. A student cuts out the booklet patterns on page 121 along the bold lines.
2. To create a booklet, the student glues the "Clouds" cutout on the first section of the strip. He then glues each cloud description on a separate section.
3. He pulls and stretches cotton balls to resemble each cloud formation described.
4. He glues each formation to its appropriate section. He uses the reference books for help, if needed.

# A Rockin' Investigation

**Skill:** Observing characteristics of rocks

**Materials needed:**
- 6 varied rocks
- a permanent marker
- a class supply of the form on page 124
- pencils
- a large container of water

**Setting up the center:**
1. Use the permanent marker to write a different number from 1 to 6 on each rock.
2. Display the rocks, forms, pencils, and container of water at a center.

**Using the center:**
1. A student chooses a rock. She observes how the rock looks and feels. She then places the rock in the container of water and observes whether it sinks or floats.
2. She records her observations on her paper.
3. She completes Steps 1–2 for each remaining rock.

# Home, Sweet Home

**Skill:** Classifying animals by habitat

**Materials needed:**
- a supply of shoeboxes
- magazine pictures of various animal habitats (desert, ocean, rain forest, arctic, woodland, etc.)
- a plastic animal or picture of an animal that can be found in each habitatat
- transparent tape
- habitat reference books
- sheet of paper
- glue
- marker

**Setting up the center:**
1. Glue each habitat picture to the interior of a different shoebox.
2. List the names of the animals for each habitat on a sheet of paper and then tape it to the bottom of the corresponding shoebox.
3. Display the boxes, books, and plastic animals or animal pictures at a center.

**Using the center:**
1. A student selects an animal (plastic or picture) and places it in the correct habitat box.
2. He continues in this manner until all of the animals have been placed.
3. He uses the reference materials for help, if needed.
4. He checks his work by looking at the list on the bottom of each box.

# Heat, Light, and Sound

**Skill:** Classifying energy sources

**Materials needed:**
- 2 copies of the cards on page 125
- three 9" x 12" sheets of construction paper
- scissors
- markers

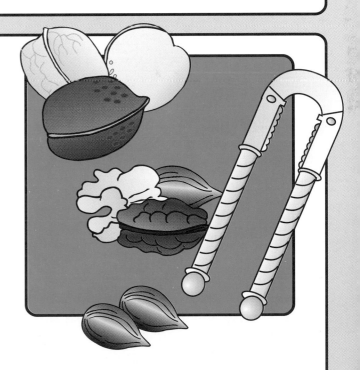

**Setting up the center:**
1. Program each sheet of construction paper with one of the following words to make three workmats: "Heat," "Light," and "Sound."
2. Color and then cut out the energy source cards on page 125.
3. Create an answer key by labeling each energy source shown with the appropriate category on the second copy of page 125.
4. Display the mats, cards, and answer key at a center.

**Using the center:**
1. A student arranges the mats and cards on a table or workspace.
2. She chooses a card, decides which type of energy it represents, and places it on the appropriate mat.
3. She continues in this manner until all the cards are placed.
4. After placing the cards, she checks her work using the answer key.

# Completely Nuts

**Skill:** Observing characteristics of nuts

**Materials needed:**
- a supply of mixed nuts with shells
- a nutcracker
- a class supply of lined paper
- pencils

**Setting up the center:**
1. Remove the shell from one of each type of nut.
2. Display the nuts with and without shells, nutcracker, paper, and pencils at a center.

**Using the center:**
1. A student examines each nut without a shell, noticing its size, weight, shape, color, and texture.
2. He cracks one of the nuts with a shell, taking notice of its size, weight, shape, color, and texture.
3. He matches each nut with a shell to a nut without a shell of the same type.
4. After pairing the nuts, he records his observations about the pair on a sheet of paper.
5. He continues in the same manner until he finds a match for each type of nut.

# Caps Galore

**Skill:** Classifying objects

**Materials needed:**
- a 9" x 12" sheet of construction paper
- 20–25 clean caps or lids from various containers
- a small box
- a class supply of lined paper
- pencils

**Setting up the center:**
1. On the sheet of construction paper, create a direction sheet like the one shown.
2. Store the caps in the box. Display the instructions, box, pencils, and paper at a center.

**Using the center:**
1. A student removes the caps from the box.
2. She completes the activity by following the directions on the sheet.
3. She displays her work in a designated area.

**Center Directions:**
Sort the caps into these groups: size, shape, color, texture, and type of cap (twist-on or press-on).

Next, think of another way to sort the caps. On a sheet of paper, tell how you sorted the caps into this new group. Draw a picture of the caps in this group.

# Science in a Bag

**Skill:** Classifying animals

**Materials needed:**
- a supply of magazines
- a supply of paper lunch bags
- scissors
- markers

**Setting up the center:**
1. Write one animal classification category on each bag. For example, label bags with "Reptiles," "Mammals," "Birds," and "Fish."
2. Display the bags, magazines, and scissors at a center.

**Using the center:**
1. A student reads the animal classification category listed on each bag.
2. He looks through the magazines for a picture to represent each one. He cuts out the picture and places it in the appropriate bag.
3. Once all students have visited the center, share the pictures from each bag with students to check for correct classification.

# Finding Fats

**Skill:** Identifying foods containing fat

**Materials needed:**
- a class supply of the "Finding Fats" form on page 126
- five 1½" brown paper bag squares for each child
- peanut butter
- a class supply of cheese curls, jelly beans, pretzel sticks, and potato chips
- a flashlight
- pencils or markers
- a stapler

**Setting up the center:**
Display the materials at a center.

**Using the center:**
1. A student predicts whether each food contains fat. She records her predictions on a form.
2. The student rubs a different food on each paper square. She then shines the flashlight against the back of each square to check for grease spots. She records the results on her form and then staples the squares in the last column.

# Creeping Colors

**Skill:** Separating secondary colors

**Materials needed:**
- purple, orange, green, and black watercolor markers
- four 1" x 6" white paper towel strips for each child
- 4 sharpened pencils
- 4 clear plastic cups, each filled with 1" of water
- a class supply of the "Creeping Colors" form on page 127
- crayons    • tape

**Setting up the center:**
Display the materials at a center.

**Using the center:**
1. A student uses a different-colored marker to make a thick line in the middle of each paper towel strip. He then labels the top of each strip with its matching color word and his initials.
2. The student gently pushes a pencil through one end of each strip until the strip hangs from the center of the pencil. He then sets each pencil across the top of a different cup so that the strip is touching the water.
3. He observes each strip for any changes and then records the results on his form.
4. The student removes the strips and sets them aside to dry. He then tapes them to the back of his form.

# Baggin' Properties

**Skill:** Identifying properties of matter (solids)

**Materials needed:**
- a permanent marker
- a shoebox
- 5 paper lunch bags, each labeled with a different property like the ones shown
- 2 or more small corresponding items for each bag

**Setting up the center:**
1. Use the marker to program the bottom of the box with each property and its matching items for self-checking. (Each item may have more than one of the indicated properties.) Store the items inside the box.
2. Display the box and bags at a center.

**Using the center:**
1. A student reads the property on each bag. She then removes an item from the box and places it in its corresponding bag.
2. After sorting all the items, she turns over the box to check her work.

# Matter Wheel

**Skill:** Identifying the three states of matter

**Materials needed:**
- a glue stick
- 8 magazine pictures (2 showing gases, 3 showing liquids, and 3 showing solids)
- a thin paper plate, sectioned as shown
- a permanent marker
- 8 spring-type clothespins
- a resealable plastic bag

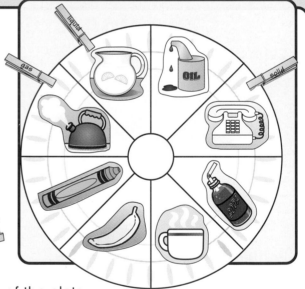

**Setting up the center:**
1. Glue each magazine picture to a different section of the plate.
2. Fold the plate to crease each line. Program each section of the paper plate back with the state of matter of the picture on the front of the plate.
3. Label each side of each clothespin: two "gas," three "liquid," and three "solid."
4. Store the clothespins in the plastic bag. Display the paper plate and bag at a center.

**Using the center:**
1. A student removes the clothespins from the bag and arranges them on a table or workspace.
2. He reads the word on each clothespin and then clips each one to its matching picture.
3. After placing all the clothespins, he turns the plate over to check his work.

# Simple Machine Sort

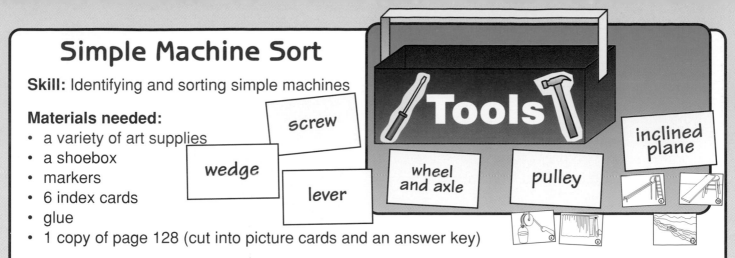

**Skill:** Identifying and sorting simple machines

**Materials needed:**
- a variety of art supplies
- a shoebox
- markers
- 6 index cards
- glue
- 1 copy of page 128 (cut into picture cards and an answer key)

**Setting up the center:**
1. Use the art supplies to decorate the box so that it resembles a toolbox.
2. Label each index card with a different type of simple machine *(wheel and axle, pulley, inclined plane, screw, wedge, and lever).*
3. Glue the answer key from page 128 on the bottom of the box.
4. Place the index cards and picture cards in the box. Display the box at a center.

**Using the center:**
1. A student removes the index cards and arranges them on a table or workspace.
2. She selects a picture card from the toolbox and then places it below its matching index card.
3. She continues in this manner until all the picture cards have been sorted.
4. She turns over the toolbox to check her answers using the key.

# Magnetic Magic

**Skill:** Identifying and sorting magnetic objects

**Materials needed:**
- transparent tape
- a disc magnet
- three 8-oz. plastic cups
- a small construction paper hat shape
- a permanent marker
- an index card
- an assortment of small magnetic and nonmagnetic items stored in a resealable plastic bag

**Setting up the center:**
1. Tape the magnet to the inside of a cup and the hat shape to the outside. Be sure the hat shape covers the magnet. Label one remaining cup "yes" and the other "no."
2. Create an answer key by listing the magnetic and nonmagnetic items on the index card.
3. Display the bag, hat, labeled cups, and answer key at a center.

**Using the center:**
1. A student removes the items from the bag and arranges them on a table or workspace.
2. He predicts whether the items are magnetic or nonmagnetic and then sorts them.
3. To check his predictions, he holds one item at a time to the front of the hat. If an item is attracted to the magnet, he places it in the "yes" cup. If it is not attracted, he places it in the "no" cup.
4. After sorting all the items, he checks his work using the answer key.

111

# Magnetic Dig

**Skill:** Identifying magnetic objects

**Materials needed:**
- the magnetic and nonmagnetic items shown on page 129
- a shallow tub half-filled with sand
- a class supply of the form on page 129, plus one extra copy
- a horseshoe magnet
- crayons

**Setting up the center:**
1. Poke the magnetic and nonmagnetic items into the sand so that they are hidden.
2. Create an answer key on the extra form by coloring the magnetic items and circling the nonmagnetic items.
3. Display the tub, forms, magnet, answer key, and crayons at the center.

**Using the center:**
1. A student gently moves the magnet through the sand until it has attracted an item.
2. She removes the item and colors the matching picture on her form. She then places the item to the side.
3. After finding all the magnetic items, she carefully removes the nonmagnetic items from the tub one at a time. She then circles each item's matching picture on the form.
4. She checks her work using the answer key.

# Make a Magnet

**Skill:** Understanding magnetism

**Materials needed:**
- a marker
- a sheet of construction paper
- a bar magnet
- a large metal paper clip
- 5 small metal paper clips

**Setting up the center:**
1. Program the sheet of construction paper as shown. Place the paper at the center to be used as a guide.
2. Display the magnet and all paper clips at the center.

**Using the center:**
1. A student reads the steps on how to complete the activity.
2. He rubs one end of the large paper clip back and forth on the magnet for at least one minute.
3. He moves the magnetized paper clip close to a small paper clip and lifts it.
4. He repeats Steps 2 and 3, each time lifting as many paper clips as he can with the magnetized paper clip.

# Weight Wisdom

**Skill:** Classifying objects according to weight

**Materials needed:**
- a variety of small items of various weights
- a supply of resealable plastic bags
- 3" x 5" index cards, folded in half
- markers

Arrange the items in order from heaviest to lightest.

**Setting up the center:**
1. Sort the items into separate resealable bags so that there are three items of various weights in each bag.
2. For each bag, program the outside of a folded card with the directions "Arrange the items in order from heaviest to lightest" or " Arrange the items in order from lightest to heaviest."
3. Write the answer key for each bag on the inside of its folded card.
4. Display the materials at a center.

**Using the center:**
1. A student removes the objects from one bag and reads the directions on the outside of the card.
2. She arranges the items in order according to the directions.
3. After arranging, she checks her work by reading the list on the inside of the folded card.

# Creation Station

**Skills:** Understanding recycling, using creative-thinking skills

**Materials needed:**
- a supply of discarded items, such as bottle caps, film canisters, buttons, and bottles
- a large box
- glue
- tape
- 3" x 5" index cards
- scissors
- pencils
- yarn

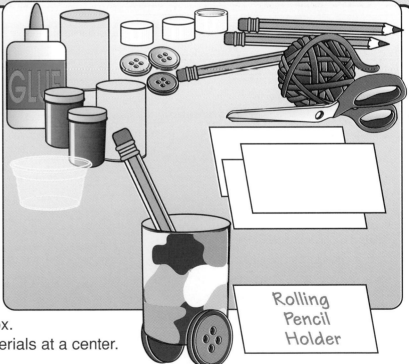

Rolling Pencil Holder

**Setting up the center:**
1. Place the discarded items in the box.
2. Display the box and remaining materials at a center.

**Using the center:**
1. A student chooses several items from the box and arranges them on the table or workspace.
2. He decides how he can combine the items to create a new invention.
3. He creates his new invention and then writes the name of his invention on an index card.
4. He places his invention and name plate in a designated display area.

# Precipitation

**Skill:** Understanding types of precipitation

**Materials needed:**
- a variety of precipitation picture books
- a class supply of the patterns on page 130
- pencils
- scissors
- a class supply of 9" x 12" sheets of blue construction paper
- glue
- hole puncher
- yarn

**Setting up the center:**
1. Create a sample mobile like the one shown.
2. Display the sample and remaining materials at a center.

**Using the center:**
1. A student reads the books to find one fact about each form of precipitation. She writes one sentence about each type on a cloud on page 130.
2. She cuts out each pattern piece and glues it onto a sheet of construction paper.
3. She again cuts out each pattern piece, leaving a narrow blue border.
4. She hole-punches where indicated and assembles her mobile as shown in the sample.
5. She hangs her project in a designated display area.

**Types of Precipitation**

Rain
Rain is the most common type of precipitation.

Sleet
Sleet usually falls in the winter.

Hail
Hail usually falls during the summer.

Snow
When a lot of heavy snow falls, it can be called a blizzard.

# Food Chain Lineup

**Skill:** Understanding a food chain

**Materials needed:**
- magazine cutouts or drawings of the items shown
- six 3" x 5" index cards
- a variety of food chain picture books
- a length of twine
- 6 clothespins
- crayons or markers
- scissors
- glue

**Setting up the center:**
1. Glue each cutout or drawing to a separate index card.
2. Label the back of each card with a number to indicate its place in the food chain (see illustration).
3. Suspend the twine above the table or workspace at a center.
4. Display the cards, clothespins, and books at the center.

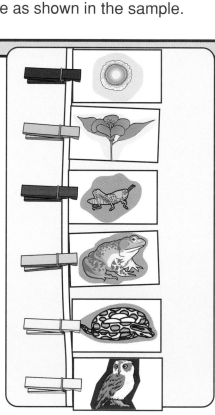

**Using the center:**
1. A student arranges the cards according to the food chain order. (He may refer to the provided books as needed.)
2. He clips each card, in order, to the clothesline.
3. After placing all the cards, he checks his work by flipping the cards over.

# Constellation Cards

**Skill:** Identifying constellations

**Materials needed:**
- a sharpened pencil
- a supply of 3" x 3" black poster board squares
- a supply of blank index cards
- a yellow highlighter

**Setting up the center:**
1. Plot the points of a desired constellation on a black square. Insert the pencil through each point to make a hole.
2. Place the black square over an index card. Plot each constellation point onto the card using the holes in the black square as a guide.
3. Connect the points on the index card. Highlight each point and write the name of the constellation at the bottom of the card. Repeat Steps 1–3 for a desired number of constellations.
4. Display the cards at a center.

**Using the center:**
1. A student chooses a black constellation card. She holds it up to the light and then finds the matching constellation on an index card.
2. She repeats the activity for the remaining cards.
3. After matching the cards, she checks her work by placing each black card over the matching index card. If she can see the stars through the holes, it is a correct match.

# Phases-of-the-Moon Wheel

**Skill:** Sequencing and naming the phases of the moon

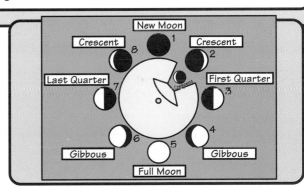

**Materials needed:**
- scissors
- a 6" paper circle
- glue
- markers
- an 11" x 14" sheet of construction paper
- a brad
- 8 paper strips, each labeled with a different moon phase
- eight 2" paper circles, each showing a different moon phase

**Setting up the center:**
1. Cut a wedge-shaped flap in the large circle as shown. Use the brad to attach the resulting wheel to the center of the construction paper.
2. Program the construction paper as shown. Glue "New Moon" strip above number 1.
3. Line up the wheel opening with the number 1. Lift the flap. Label the space "New Moon" and illustrate this phase. Repeat this step for each consecutive phase.
4. Display the wheel, paper circles, and strips at a center.

**Using the center:**
1. A student places the moon-phase circles, in sequence, around the wheel.
2. He places the strip labeled with the name of the moon phase beside the picture phase.
3. After placing all the circles, he checks his work by lining up the wheel and lifting the flap.

# Will It Flow?

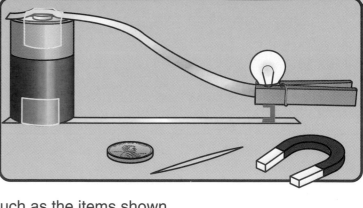

**Skill:** Identifying conductors and insulators

**Materials needed:**
- transparent tape
- two 8" strips of aluminum foil
- 1 D battery
- 1 flashlight bulb
- 1 clothespin
- a supply of metal and nonmetal test items, such as the items shown
- a class supply of the "Will It Flow" form on page 131

**Setting up the center:**
1. Tape one end of a strip of aluminum foil to each end of the battery.
2. Wrap the opposite end of the top strip of foil around the metal end of the bulb and attach the clothespin as shown.
3. Display the resulting electrical circuit, test items, and forms at a center.

**Using the center:**
1. A student chooses an object and predicts whether it will conduct electricity. She records her information on the form.
2. To test her prediction, she places the object on the foil and the bottom of the lightbulb on top of the object as shown. She records the results of the experiment on the form.
4. The student completes Steps 1–2 for each remaining item.

# Five Senses Collage

**Skill:** Recognizing the five senses

**Materials needed:**
- a class supply of 11" x 14" sheets of construction paper
- a supply of magazines
- scissors
- glue
- markers
- pencils

**Setting up the center:**
Display the materials at a center.

**Using the center:**
1. The student uses markers to draw a face (including eyes, ears, nose, and mouth) and hands on a sheet of construction paper.
2. He cuts out a magazine picture that illustrates a use for each of the five senses.
3. The student glues the pictures to the appropriate area on the construction paper and on the back of this sheet writes a sentence about how he uses each sense.

# Rotate and Revolve

**Skill:** Recognizing the earth's movements

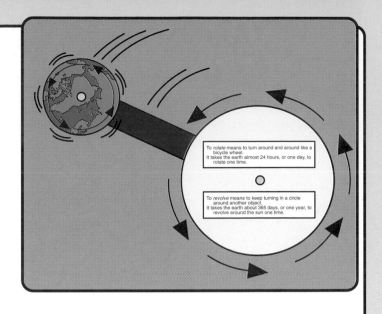

**Materials needed:**
- a class supply of white construction paper copies of page 132
- crayons
- glue
- scissors
- a supply of brads
- a supply of 1" x 8" poster board strips that have been hole-punched on each end

**Setting up the center:**

Display the materials at a center.

**Using the center:**
1. A student colors the earth and sun patterns on page 132 and then cuts them out, along with the earth movement fact cards.
2. She glues the facts to the sun pattern.
3. She uses brads to fasten the cutouts to the ends of a poster board strip programmed as shown.
4. The student reads the "Rotate" fact and moves the earth to make it rotate. She then reads the "Revolve" fact and moves the earth to make it revolve around the sun.
5. When all students have completed the center, lead the group to use their models to show how the earth rotates as it revolves around the sun.

# Nine Little Planets

**Skill:** Ordering the planets

| Mercury | Venus | Earth | Mars | Jupiter | Saturn | Uranus | Neptune | Pluto |
|---------|-------|-------|------|---------|--------|--------|---------|-------|

### Clues

Mars is known as the Red Planet. It is the fourth planet.
Venus is the hottest planet. It comes right after Mercury.
Saturn is known for its bright rings. It is the sixth planet.
Earth is our home planet. It comes right before Mars.
Mercury is the second smallest planet. It is first in line.
Pluto is the smallest planet. It is the farthest from the sun.
Uranus orbits on its side. It comes right after Saturn.
Neptune is a dark and icy planet. It is the eighth planet.
Jupiter is the largest planet. It comes right before the bright-ringed planet.

**Materials needed:**
- a copy of the planet cards and clues on page 133
- scissors
- marker
- manila envelope

**Setting up the center:**
1. Cut apart the planet cards and clues along the dashed lines.
2. List the planets in order on the back of the clue card to create an answer key.
3. Store the cards in the envelope.
4. Display the envelope at a center.

**Using the center:**
1. A student removes the planet cards and clues from the envelope and then arranges them on a table or workspace.
2. He reads the clues and then places the planet cards in the correct order.
3. After placing all the cards, he checks his work by looking at the answer key on the back of the clue card.

# Four Seasons Box

**Skill:** Identifying seasonal characteristics

**Materials needed:**
- a large box covered with bulletin board paper as shown
- markers
- a supply of magazines or catalogs
- scissors
- glue

**Setting up the center:**
1. Write one season name on each side of the box.
2. Display the box, magazines, scissors, and glue at a center.

**Using the center:**
1. A student looks through the magazines or catalogs for pictures of items that represent each season, such as the following: snowy weather (winter), a colorful flower (spring), the beach (summer), a pumpkin (fall).
2. She cuts out the pictures and then glues them to the side of the box labeled with the appropriate season.
3. After all students have visited the center, allow each child to share her chosen pictures and explain the seasons they represent.

# See the Sound

**Skill:** Understanding sound vibrations

**Materials needed:**
- a 9" x 12" sheet of construction paper
- a marker
- a class supply of large yellow balloons
- a small amount of rice in a container
- a class supply of lined paper
- pencils

All sounds are made by the vibrations of an object. When a sound is made, the air or surrounding matter begins to vibrate. The vibrations then travel away from the object.

**Setting up the center:**
1. On the construction paper, write the sound facts as shown.
2. Display the sound facts, balloons, rice, paper, and pencils at a center.

**Using the center:**
1. A student takes a balloon and puts 10–12 grains of rice in it.
2. He blows up the balloon until the latex is thin and easy to see through. Then he ties the neck of the balloon in a knot. (Assist children who need help tying the knot.)
3. He holds the balloon on its side and then talks or sings with his mouth against the balloon's surface.
4. As he speaks, he watches through the balloon for movement of the rice.
5. On a sheet of lined paper, he writes why he thinks the rice moved inside the balloon.

# Sink or Float

**Skill:** Determining whether objects sink or float

**Materials needed:**
- an assortment of objects that either float or sink (an equal number of each)
- a large resealable plastic bag
- a shallow tub half-filled with water
- a class supply of paper, folded lengthwise
- pencils

**Setting up the center:**
1. Store the objects in the plastic bag.
2. Display the bag, tub, paper, and pencils at a center.

**Using the center:**
1. A student removes the items from the bag and arranges them on a table or workspace.
2. She labels one side of a sheet of paper "sink" and the other side "float."
3. She puts one item in the water and observes whether it sinks or floats. She then records the results on her paper.
4. The student removes the item from the water and sets it aside.
5. She continues in this manner until all the objects have been tested.

# Heat All Around

**Skill:** Identifying natural and man-made heat sources

**Materials needed:**
- markers
- 2 paper lunch bags
- an assortment of pictures of natural and man-made heat sources
- a resealable plastic bag

**Setting up the center:**
1. Program each paper bag as shown.
2. Program the bottom of each paper bag with the corresponding picture names for self-checking.
3. Store the pictures in the plastic bag. Display the plastic and paper bags at a center.

**Using the center:**
1. A student removes the pictures from the plastic bag and arranges them on a table or workspace.
2. He selects a picture and decides whether it illustrates a natural or a man-made heat source. The student places it in its corresponding bag.
3. After sorting all the pictures, he removes them from the bags and checks his work using the answer keys.

# Cube Pattern

Use with "Animal Blocks" on page 100.

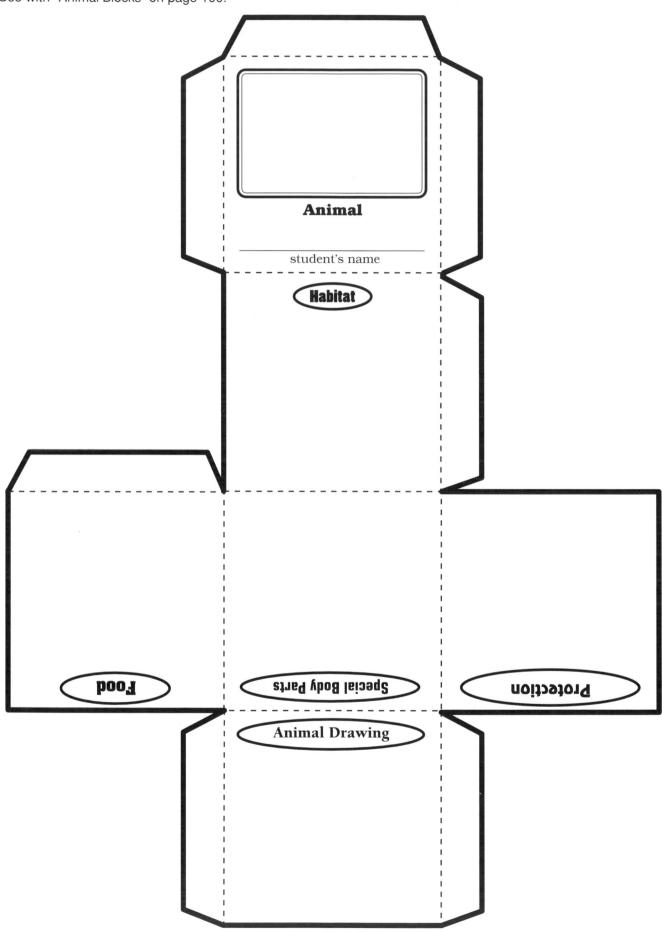

Animal

student's name

Habitat

Food

Special Body Parts

Protection

Animal Drawing

Name _____

# Build-a-Bug Checklist
After you build your bug, check off each body part that your bug has.

☐ head
☐ thorax
☐ abdomen
☐ antennae
☐ eyes
☐ legs
☐ wings (if any)

**Note to the teacher:** Use with "Build a Bug" on page 100.

## Booklet Patterns
Use with "Partly Cloudy, Partly Cotton" on page 105.

**Clouds**

**Cirrus** clouds are thin and feathery. These clouds are made of ice crystals. Cirrus clouds are found very high in the sky.

**Cumulus** clouds are puffy piles of clouds. They may change into clouds called *thunderheads.* The bottoms of cumulus clouds can be seen low in the sky.

**Stratus** clouds look like thick, even blankets in the sky. Sometimes rain or snow falls from them. Stratus clouds are found low in the sky.

# Insect Cards and Insect Information Card

Use with "Is It a Helper? Is It a Pest?" on page 101.

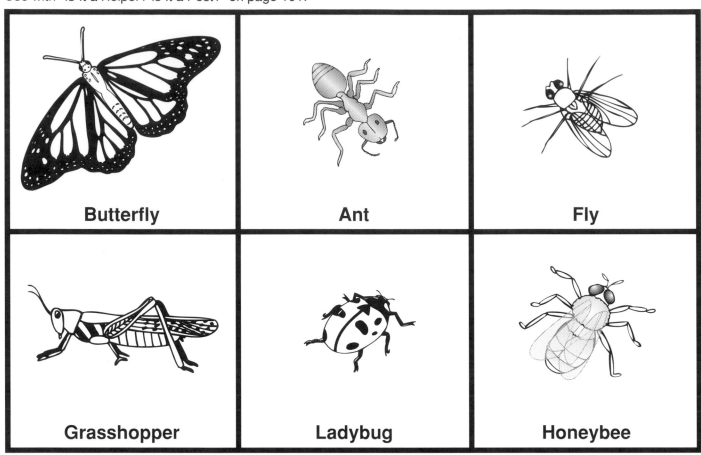

Butterfly

Ant

Fly

Grasshopper

Ladybug

Honeybee

## Insect Information Card

- **Butterflies** help flowers reproduce by carrying pollen from flower to flower.
- **Honeybees** pollinate crops and produce honey.
- Some **grasshoppers** eat plants. In fact, they may destroy whole crops of alfalfa, cotton, and corn.
- **Ants** kill insects that may damage crops. They also dig underground, which improves the soil by breaking it up. However, some ants protect aphids and other insects that may harm crops.
- Some **flies** carry germs inside their bodies, in the tips of their mouthparts, or on the hairs on their bodies. Some of these germs can cause serious diseases in plants and animals.
- One **ladybug** may eat as much as 100 aphids a day. Aphids are insects that destroy crops by sucking the juice out of plants.

Name _____

*Foliage Fun*

**Toothed Edge**

**Lobed Edge**

**Smooth Edge**

**Palmate Vein Pattern**

**Pinnate Vein Pattern**

Name _____ *Recording observations*

# A Rockin' Investigation

| | How does the rock look? | How does the rock feel? | Does the rock sink or float? |
|---|---|---|---|
| **1** | | | |
| **2** | | | |
| **3** | | | |
| **4** | | | |
| **5** | | | |
| **6** | | | |

**Fun Fact Question:** There is only one kind of rock that floats. What is it called?

**Note to the teacher:** Use with "A Rockin' Investigtion" on page 106. **Answer to Fun Fact Question:** pumice

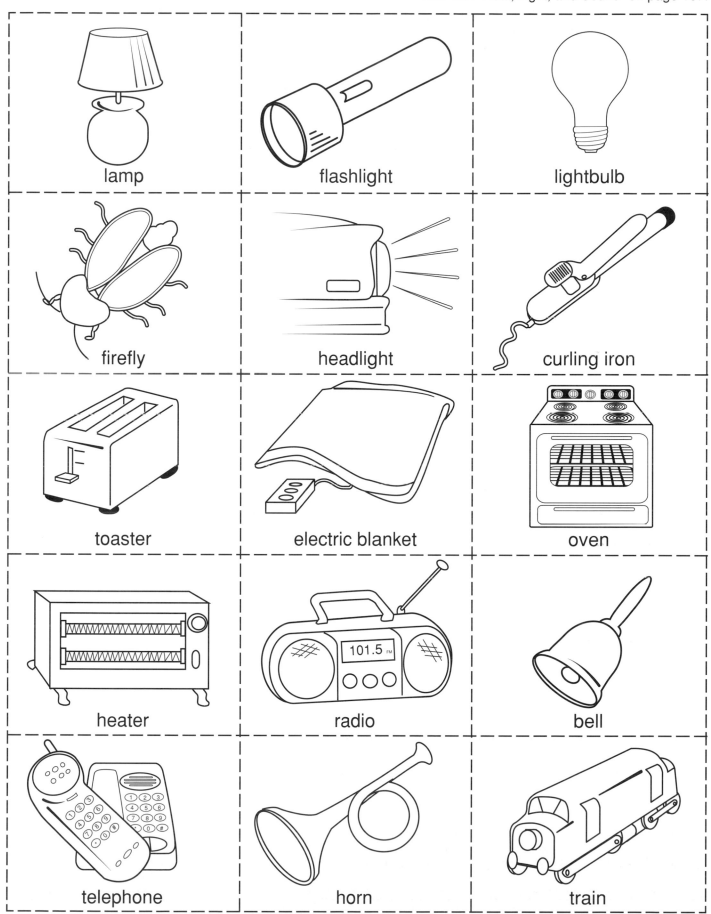

lamp

flashlight

lightbulb

firefly

headlight

curling iron

toaster

electric blanket

oven

heater

radio

bell

telephone

horn

train

Name _____

     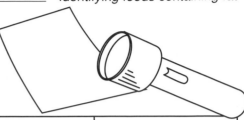

# Finding Fats

| Foods | Prediction: Do you think it contains fat? Explain. | Results: Does it seem to contain fat? Explain. | My Squares |
|---|---|---|---|
| Peanut Butter | | | |
| Cheese Curls | | | |
| Jelly Beans | | | |
| Pretzel Sticks | | | |
| Potato Chips | | | |

**Note to the teacher:** Use with "Finding Fats" on page 109.

# Creeping Colors

Color to show what happened.
Write what happened.

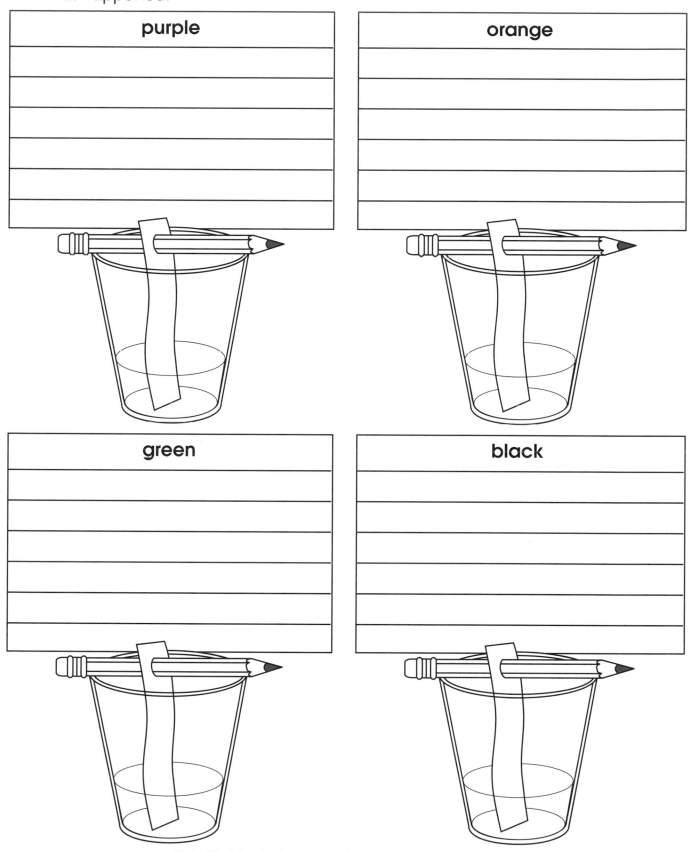

| purple |
| --- |

| orange |
| --- |

| green |
| --- |

| black |
| --- |

**Note to the teacher:** Use with "Creeping Colors" on page 109.

# Simple Machine Cards

Use with "Simple Machine Sort" on page 111.

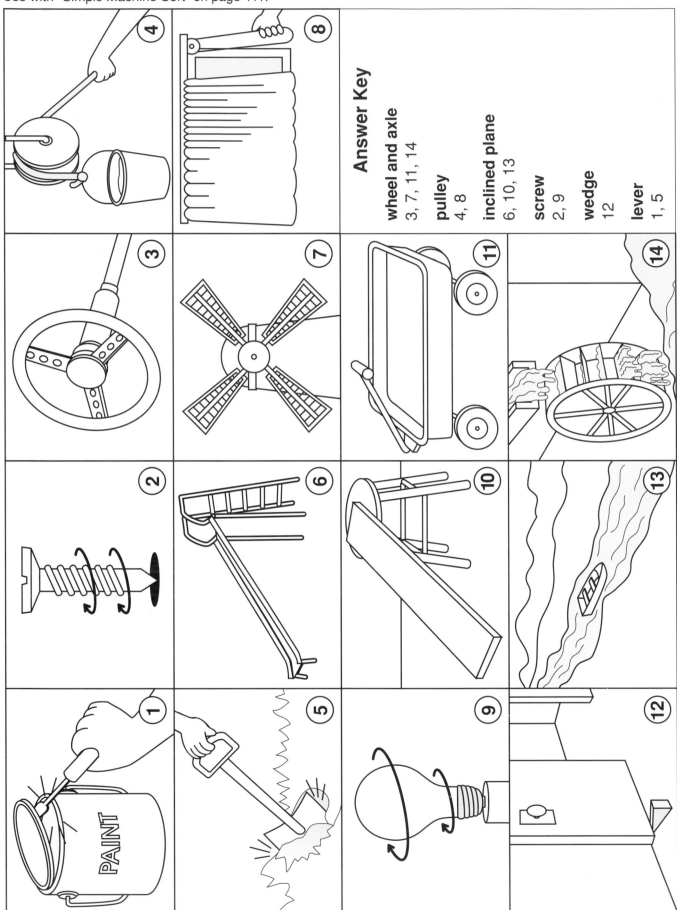

**Answer Key**

**wheel and axle**
3, 7, 11, 14

**pulley**
4, 8

**inclined plane**
6, 10, 13

**screw**
2, 9

**wedge**
12

**lever**
1, 5

# Magnificent Magnetic Dig

Color the items that are
attracted to the magnet.
Circle the items that are
not attracted to it.

Magnet
Power!

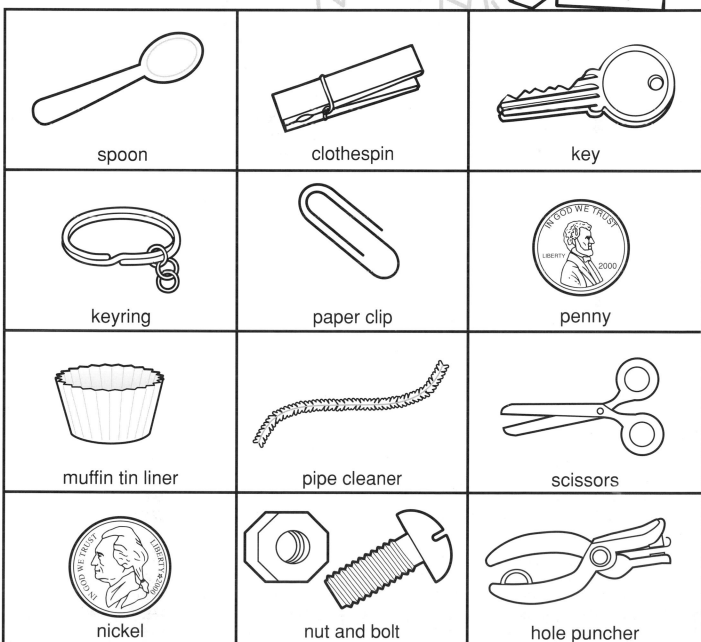

| | | |
|---|---|---|
| spoon | clothespin | key |
| keyring | paper clip | penny |
| muffin tin liner | pipe cleaner | scissors |
| nickel | nut and bolt | hole puncher |

**Note to the teacher:** Use with "Magnetic Dig" on page 112.

**Precipitation Patterns**
Use with "Precipitation" on page 114.

# Types of Precipitation

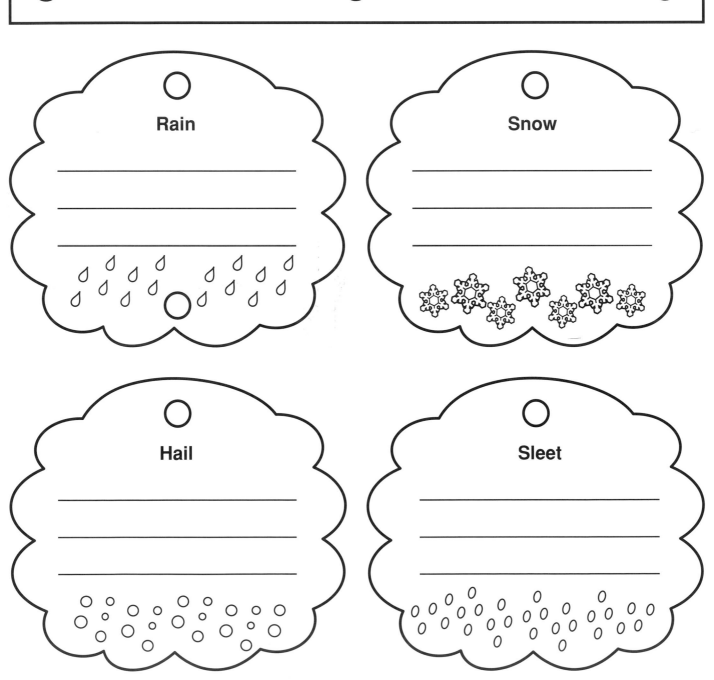

Rain

Snow

Hail

Sleet

# Will It Flow?

*Conductors* let electricity flow. *Insulators* do not let electricity flow. Follow the directions below to see if the objects you have chosen will let the electricity flow!

**Directions:**
1. List the objects.
2. Record your predictions. Write C for conductor and I for insulator.
3. Test your predictions. If the bulb lights, the item is a conductor.
   If the bulb does not light, the item is an insulator.
4. Record your results. Write C for conductor
   and I for insulator.

| Object | Prediction | Result |
|--------|------------|--------|
|        |            |        |
|        |            |        |
|        |            |        |
|        |            |        |
|        |            |        |
|        |            |        |
|        |            |        |
|        |            |        |

# Earth and Sun Patterns

Use patterns and cards with "Rotate and Revolve" on page 117.

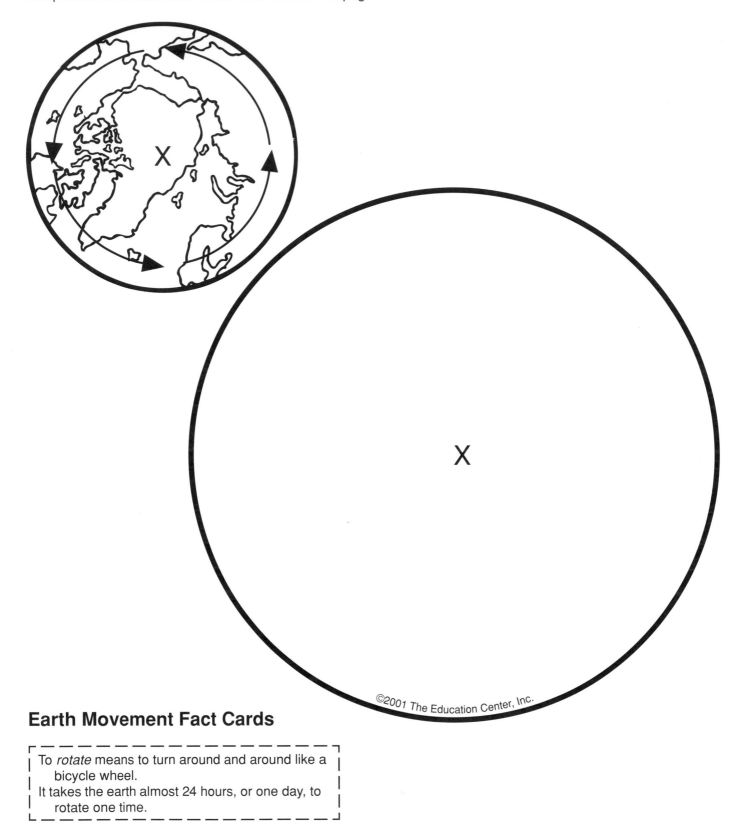

©2001 The Education Center, Inc.

## Earth Movement Fact Cards

To *rotate* means to turn around and around like a
   bicycle wheel.
It takes the earth almost 24 hours, or one day, to
   rotate one time.

To *revolve* means to keep turning in a circle
   around another object.
It takes the earth about 365 days, or one year, to
   revolve around the sun one time.

©2001 The Education Center, Inc. • *Sensational Centers* • TEC2869

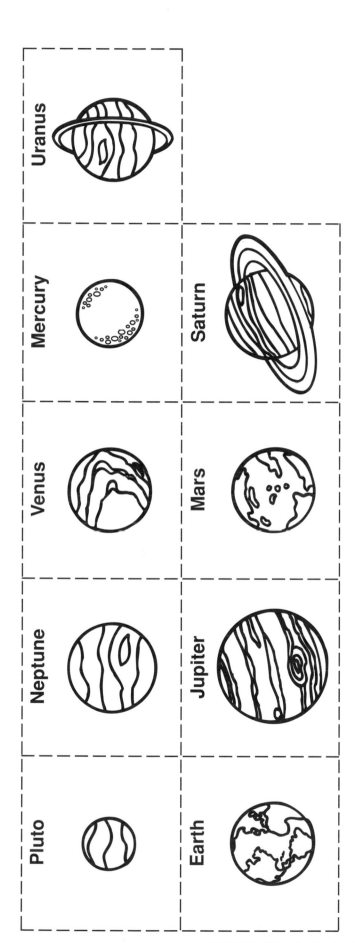

## Clues

**Mars** is known as the Red Planet. It is the fourth planet.

**Venus** is the hottest planet. It comes right after Mercury.

**Saturn** is known for its bright rings. It is the sixth planet.

**Earth** is our home planet. It comes right before Mars.

**Mercury** is the second-smallest planet. It is first in line.

**Pluto** is the smallest planet. It is the farthest from the sun.

**Uranus** orbits on its side. It comes right after Saturn.

**Neptune** is a dark and icy planet. It is the eighth planet.

**Jupiter** is the largest planet. It comes right before the bright-ringed planet.

# Holiday & Seasonal

# Back-to-School Timeline of Mine

**Skill:** Sequencing events

**Materials needed:**
- 6 index cards for each student (plus 1 extra set of 6)
- a class supply of resealable plastic bags (plus 1 extra)
- a basket or other container
- markers or crayons
- pencils

**Setting up the center:**
1. Create a sample set of timeline cards by following Steps 1–3 below.
2. Display the basket and remaining materials at a center.

**Using the center:**
1. A student writes a description and date of a personal event on each of six index cards. If desired, the student draws a corresponding picture of each event.
2. She arranges the cards in chronological order and then numbers the backs of the cards sequentially.
3. She writes her name on a bag, places her cards inside, and then stores the bag in the basket.
4. She then chooses a different bag from the basket. She removes the cards and arranges them in order from the earliest to the most recent event listed.
5. If time allows, she may choose another bag from the basket.

# ABC Backpack

**Skill:** Alphabetizing

**Materials needed:**
- 1 backpack
- a variety of school supplies, such as a pencil, an eraser, a ruler, etc.
- a permanent marker
- a supply of index cards
- masking tape

**Setting up the center:**
1. Use masking tape to label each item with its name. (Tape smaller items to index cards and label the cards.)
2. Place each item in the backpack.
3. To create an answer key, write "School Supplies" on one side of an index card and then list the items in alphabetical order on the reverse side.
4. Display the backpack and answer key card at a center.

**Using the center:**
1. A student removes the items from the backpack and places them on a table or workspace.
2. He arranges the items in alphabetical order.
3. After arranging the items, the student turns the index card over to check his work.

# Autumn Vowels

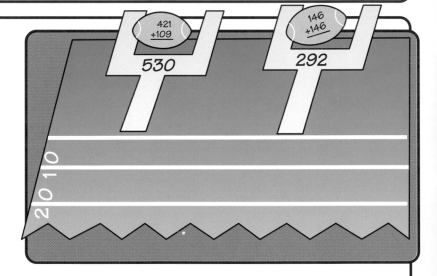

**Skill:** Identifying vowel sounds

**Materials needed:**
- 5 red construction paper leaf cutouts
- a permanent marker
- 10 yellow construction paper leaf cutouts
- a small plastic pail
- transparent tape
- a child's small plastic rake

**Setting up the center:**
1. Program each red leaf cutout with a vowel sound.
2. Program each yellow leaf cutout with a word containing one of the vowel sounds.
3. Write the corresponding vowel sound on the back of each yellow leaf. Store these leaves in the pail.
4. Tape the red leaves, leaving several inches between each one, to a tabletop at a center. Display the rake and pail at the center.

**Using the center:**
1. A student empties the yellow leaves onto the table or workspace.
2. She reads the word on each yellow leaf. She then "rakes" each yellow leaf onto the red leaf containing its matching vowel sound.
3. After raking all of the leaves, the student turns over each yellow leaf to check her work.

# Touchdown Math

**Skill:** Solving math facts

**Materials needed:**
- a supply of football-shaped cutouts
- a marker
- 8 goalpost-shaped cutouts
- one 12" x 18" sheet of green construction paper labeled as shown
- a class supply of lined paper
- pencils

**Setting up the center:**
1. Program each football cutout with a different math fact, making sure there are only eight different answers in all. Write the correct answer on the back of each football.
2. Write each answer on a goalpost cutout. Laminate the cutouts for durability, if desired.
4. Display the cutouts and the construction paper football field at a center.

**Using the center:**
1. A student lays four goalposts at each end of the football field. He spreads the footballs, equation side up, across the field.
2. He chooses a football and then solves the equation on a sheet of paper. He then places the football in between the posts of the goal containing the corresponding answer.
3. After placing each football, the student turns the footballs over to check his work.

# Synonym Pumpkins

**Skill:** Identifying synonyms

**Materials needed:**
- a copy of synonym pumpkin patterns on page 165
- a permanent marker
- a thesaurus
- a dry-erase marker
- a paper towel

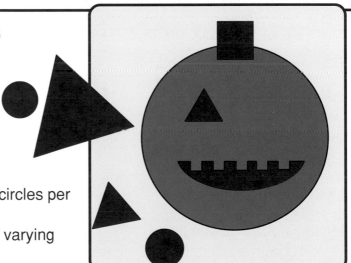

**Setting up the center:**
1. Choose a desired number of synonym word pairs. Program each pumpkin lid with one word from each pair.
2. Write the matching synonym on the back of each pumpkin, and then laminate.
3. Display the laminated pumpkin sheet and the remaining materials at a center.

**Using the center:**
1. A student reads the word on each pumpkin lid.
2. She uses the thesaurus to find a synonym for each word.
3. The student uses the dry-erase marker to write a synonym on the mouth of each pumpkin.
4. After completing all the synonym word pairs, the student turns the sheet over to check her work. Then she uses the paper towel to erase her answers.

# Pumpkin Partners

**Skill:** Following directions

**Materials needed:**
- 2 resealable plastic bags
- two 9" orange construction paper circles
- 2 small and 2 large black construction paper triangles per plastic bag
- 2 small and 2 large black construction paper circles per plastic bag
- 1 set of 3 black construction paper mouths of varying sizes and shapes per plastic bag

**Setting up the center:**
Display the orange circles and the filled bags at a center.

**Using the center:**
1. Two students sit back-to-back, each with an orange circle and a bag.
2. One student places a shape from the bag onto his orange circle. Then he names the shape and its placement to his partner.
3. Using his own set of materials, the partner then places the shape on his orange circle.
4. After creating complete pumpkin faces, partners compare their work. If time allows, partners may switch roles and repeat the activity.

# "Spook-tacular" Speech

**Skill:** Identifying nouns and verbs

**Materials needed:**
- two 16 oz. cups
- a permanent marker
- a supply of construction paper cutouts in seasonal shapes
- a supply of drinking straws
- transparent tape

**Setting up the center:**
1. Label one cup "nouns" and the other cup "verbs."
2. Program the front of each cutout with an underlined noun or verb used in a sentence. Then program the back top portion of each cutout with the correct part of speech for self-checking.
3. Tape a straw to the back of each cutout.
4. Display the cups and cutouts at a center.

**Using the center:**
1. A student reads the sentence on each cutout and determines the part of speech of the underlined word.
2. She places each straw in the correct cup.
3. After placing all the cutouts, the student turns them over to check her work.

# Pumpkin Puzzlers

**Skill:** Practicing math facts

**Materials needed:**
- a supply of candy corn cutouts
- markers
- scissors
- a pumpkin-shaped plastic container (or other container)

**Setting up the center:**
1. Program each candy corn cutout with a desired math fact on the top half and its answer on the bottom half.
2. Label the back of each top half with the correct answer. Laminate the cutouts for durability, if desired.
3. Puzzle-cut each of the cutouts, and then place it in the container.
4. Display the container at a center.

**Using the center:**
1. A student removes the puzzle pieces from the pumpkin and arranges them on a table or workspace.
2. He reads each math fact and matches it with the corresponding answer.
3. After matching all the pieces, the student turns over the top halves to check his work.

# Welcome to My Web

**Skill:** Identifying odd and even numbers

**Materials needed:**
- a supply of tagboard spider cutouts
- a resealable plastic bag
- 2 half sheets of tagboard, each decorated with a spiderweb and labeled as shown
- a marker
- self-adhesive Velcro® dots

**Setting up the center:**
1. Program each spider cutout with a desired number.
2. On the back of each web, list the corresponding numbers shown on the spider cutouts.
3. Attach the loop half of a Velcro dot to the back of each spider and a corresponding hook half to its correct web. Place the spiders in the plastic bag.
4. Display the bag and webs at a center.

**Using the center:**
1. A student removes the spiders from the bag and places them on the table or workspace.
2. She reads the numbers on the spiders and then attaches each spider to its correct web.
3. After matching all the spiders, the student turns over each web to check her work.

# Halloween Sets

**Skill:** Practicing multiplication facts

**Materials needed:**
- a class supply of paper strips
- a class supply of small paper trick-or-treat bags
- stapler
- a basket
- a class supply of drawing paper
- markers or crayons

**Setting up the center:**
1. Program each strip of paper with a desired multiplication fact.
2. Place one strip inside each bag and staple it closed. Place the bags in the basket.
3. Create a sample math-fact drawing on a piece of paper.
4. Display the basket, sample drawing, drawing paper, and markers or crayons at a center.

**Using the center:**
1. A student selects and then opens a bag, removing the multiplication fact from inside.
2. He copies the math fact and then illustrates it on a piece of drawing paper, using only Halloween symbols as shown on the sample.
3. If desired, compile the completed drawings into a multiplication fact book.

# An ABC Thanksgiving Meal

**Skill:** Alphabetizing

**Materials needed:**
- a supply of Thanksgiving-food pictures
- a supply of paper plates
- glue
- markers
- a manila folder
- a plastic dish drainer

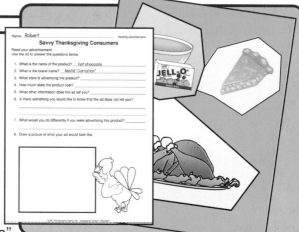

**Setting up the center:**
1. Glue each food picture to a different plate. Label each plate with its food item's name.
2. Title the front of the folder "Menu." Create an answer key by listing the food items in alphabetical order on the back of the folder.
3. Display the dish drainer, plates, and folder at a center.

**Using the center:**
1. A student arranges the plates on a table or workspace. She reads the item listed on each plate and then places the plates in alphabetical order in the dish drainer.
2. After placing all of the plates in the drainer, the student checks her work using the answer key.

# Thanksgiving Consumers

**Skill:** Reading advertisements

**Materials needed:**
- a supply of grocery store circulars featuring Thanksgiving foods
- scissors
- a supply of construction paper
- glue
- a class supply of the "Savvy Thanksgiving Consumers" form on page 166
- pencils

**Setting up the center:**
1. Cut out advertisements of Thanksgiving products familiar to the students.
2. Glue the advertisements onto the construction paper.
3. Display the ads, forms, and pencils at a center.

**Using the center:**
1. A student reads the ads and then selects an item for Thanksgiving dinner.
2. He writes the name of his food choice at the top of page 166. He then follows the directions on the page to complete the activity.
3. If time allows, the student may select another food item and repeat the activity on a separate sheet of paper.

# Traveling Tom Turkey

**Skill:** Practicing map skills

**Materials needed:**
- 12 envelopes
- a marker
- 12 index cards
- a cornucopia basket or other container
- a U.S. map
- pencils
- 12 turkey-feather cutouts

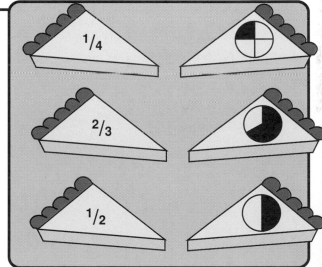

**Setting up the center:**
1. Program each envelope with the word *state* and a number between 1 and 12.
2. List two clues for each state on an index card, and then label the back of each card with the state's name for self-checking.
3. Place each card in an envelope. Then store each envelope in the basket.
4. Display the basket and remaining materials at a center.

**Using the center:**
1. A student selects an envelope and reads the clues written on the index card.
2. She uses the clues and map to identify the state's name.
3. She then writes the state's name on a turkey-feather cutout.
4. The student selects another envelope and repeats the activity for a predetermined number of times.
5. She checks her work by turning over the cards.

# Pumpkin-Pie Parts

**Skill:** Identifying fractions

**Materials needed:**
- a supply of construction paper pumpkin-pie slices
- markers
- a clean, empty pie pan

**Setting up the center:**
1. Program half of the pie slices with desired fractions.
2. Draw a corresponding answer as a shaded pie wheel on each remaining slice. Label the back of each pie-wheel slice with the correct fraction for self-checking.
3. Store the pie slices in the pie pan.
4. Display the pie pan at a center.

**Using the center:**
1. A student places the pie slices on the table or workspace, separating the pieces into written fraction slices and pie-wheel slices.
2. He reads each fraction and matches it to the correct pie-wheel slice.
3. After matching all the slices, the student turns over each pie-wheel slice to check his work.

# Mitten Matchup

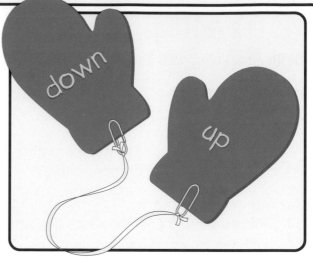

**Skill:** Matching antonyms

**Materials needed:**
- a supply of blue felt
- scissors
- a sheet of paper
- a marker
- a glitter pen
- 5 lengths of ¼" wide ribbon
- 10 paper clips
- a resealable plastic bag

**Setting up the center:**
1. Cut ten matching mitten shapes out of the felt.
2. List five pairs of antonyms on a sheet of paper.
   Use the glitter pen to write one word from each pair on each of a pair of matching mittens.
3. Tie each end of each ribbon to a different paper clip.
4. Store the mittens and ribbons in the bag. Display the bag at a center.

**Using the center:**
1. A student removes the mittens and ribbons from the bag. She reads each mitten and then matches each one to its corresponding antonym.
2. She then clips each matching antonym on either end of one ribbon. She checks her work using the list.
3. If time allows, she writes sentences using the antonyms.

# Wintry Words

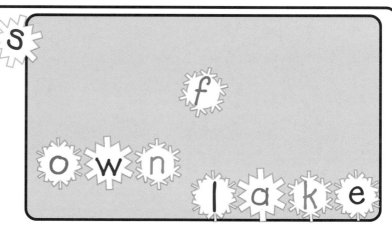

**Skill:** Building words

**Materials needed:**
- 9 construction paper snowflake cutouts
- markers
- pencils
- paper

**Setting up the center:**
1. Program each cutout with one letter from the word *snowflake.* If desired, laminate the cutouts for durability.
2. Display the snowflakes, pencils, and paper at a center.
3. Arrange the snowflakes so that they form the word *snowflake.*

**Using the center:**
1. A student takes note of the letters in the word *snowflake.* He arranges some or all of the letters to form a new word. He then copies the words on his paper.
2. He continues in the same manner, making as many words as time allows.

# FACT FLURRIES

**Skill:** Practicing addition facts to 18

**Materials needed:**
- 9 iridescent pipe cleaners cut into 2" pieces
- scissors
- twelve 3" x 5" cards
- markers

**Setting up the center:**
1. Twist three pieces of pipe cleaner together to make a snowflake as shown. Continue in this manner to make 18 snowflakes.
2. Program each card with a different addition fact with a sum no larger than 18.
3. Draw the correct number of snowflakes on the back of each card for student self-checking.
4. Display the snowflakes and cards at a center.

**Using the center:**
1. A student chooses a card and arranges the snowflakes according to the numbers on the card. She then counts to find the total number of snowflakes.
2. She checks her work by turning over the cards.

# SNOWMAN GLYPHS

**Skill:** Following directions

**Materials needed:**
- a class supply of 3", 4", and 5" white construction paper circles
- glue
- a class supply of "Snowman Decorations" on page 167
- a supply of construction paper scraps
- scissors
- crayons
- pencils

**Setting up the center:**
Display the materials at a center.

**Using the center:**
1. A student chooses one circle in each size and glues them together to form a snowman.
2. He follows the directions on page 167 to make decorations for his snowman. He glues the decorations on the snowman.
3. He colors his snowman as desired and then displays his work in a designated area.

# Hanukkah ABC

**Skill:** Alphabetizing

**Materials needed:**
- a supply of wooden clothespins
- a list of current vocabulary or spelling words in alphabetical order
- a permanent marker
- a resealable plastic bag
- a tagboard menorah cutout

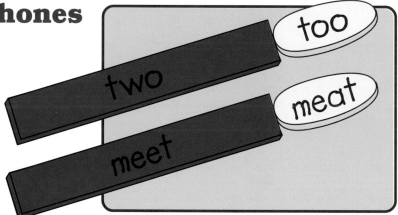

**Setting up the center:**
1. Program each clothespin with a different word from the list.
2. Store the clothespins in the bag.
3. Display the bag, menorah, and list at a center.

**Using the center:**
1. A student removes the clothespins from the bag and places them on a table or workspace.
2. The student reads the word on each clothespin.
3. She chooses nine clothespins and arranges them in alphabetical order. Then she clips each one, in turn, to the top of the menorah cutout. She checks her work using the list.
4. If time allows, she repeats the steps with nine more clothespins.

# Hanukkah Homophones

**Skill:** Identifying homophones

**Materials needed:**
- one 6" x 10" piece of red felt
- one 2" x 10" piece of yellow felt
- scissors
- a sheet of paper
- a permanent marker
- a resealable plastic bag

**Setting up the center:**
1. Cut the red felt into ten six-inch-long strips. Cut the yellow felt into ten two-inch-long flames.
2. List ten homophone word pairs on a sheet of paper.
3. Pair each candle cutout with a flame cutout. Program each candle with one word from a matching homophone pair. Program each flame with a corresponding word from each pair.
4. Place the candles and flames in the bag.
5. Display the bag and list at a center.

**Using the center:**
1. A student removes the candles and flames from the bag and places them on a table or workspace.
2. He reads each word and matches the homophone pairs by placing each flame at the top of the appropriate candle. He checks his work using the list.

# Spin the Dreidel

**Skill:** Using tally marks

**Materials needed:**
- a dreidel
- a class supply of "Spin the Dreidel" form page 168
- pencils

**Setting up the center:**
Display the materials at a center.

**Using the center:**
A student follows the directions on page 168.

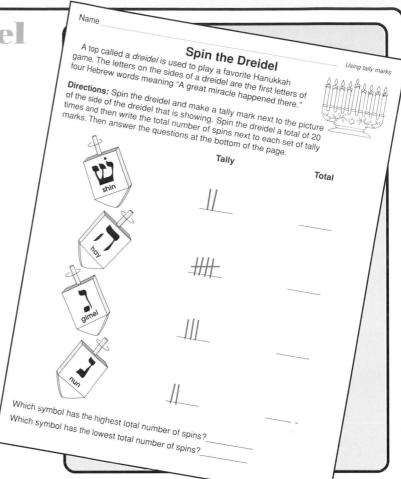

Name _____

## Spin the Dreidel

*Using tally marks*

A top called a *dreidel* is used to play a favorite Hanukkah game. The letters on the sides of a dreidel are the first letters of four Hebrew words meaning "A great miracle happened there."

**Directions:** Spin the dreidel and make a tally mark next to the picture of the side of the dreidel that is showing. Spin the dreidel a total of 20 times and then write the total number of spins next to each set of tally marks. Then answer the questions at the bottom of the page.

| | Tally | Total |
|---|---|---|
| shin | \|\| | ____ |
| hay | \|\|\|\| | ____ |
| gimel | \|\|\| | ____ |
| nun | \|\| | ____ |

Which symbol has the highest total number of spins? ____
Which symbol has the lowest total number of spins? ____

# Menorah Math

**Skill:** Identifying addition and subtraction facts

**Materials needed:**
- 27 construction paper candle cutouts
- markers
- glue
- 3 construction paper menorah cutouts

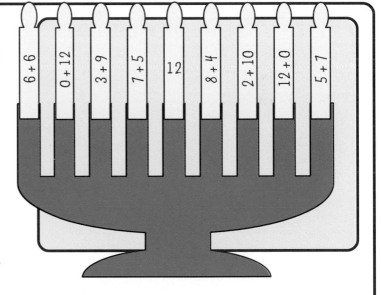

**Setting up the center:**
1. Program each of three candles with a different sum or difference. Glue one of these candles on the center candleholder of each menorah.
2. For each sum or difference, program each of eight candles with a different addition or subtraction fact that matches it.
3. Program the back of each menorah with the corresponding number sentences.
4. Display the candles and the menorahs at a center.

**Using the center:**
1. A student reads the problem on each candle and places it on the menorah with the matching sum or difference.
2. After placing all of the candles, he turns over each menorah to check his work.

145

# Stocking Stuffer Blends

**Skill:** Matching blends and rimes to make words

**Materials needed:**
- 5 construction paper stocking cutouts
- 20 construction paper candy cane cutouts
- markers
- a class supply of paper
- pencils

**Setting up the center:**
1. Program each stocking with a blend, such as *sn, br,* or *pl.*
2. Program each candy cane with two blank lines followed by a rime, such as *ap, ush,* or *ell.*
3. Display the candy canes, stockings, paper, and pencils at a center.

**Using the center:**
1. A student chooses a candy cane and matches it to a stocking to make a word. She records the word on her paper.
2. She continues in the same manner until she has matched each candy cane to a stocking.

# Reindeer Roundup

**Skill:** Matching synonyms

**Materials needed:**
- 12 empty toilet paper tubes
- 12 black pipe cleaners
- 12 pairs of wiggle eyes
- 12 small red pom-poms
- markers
- a sheet of white construction paper

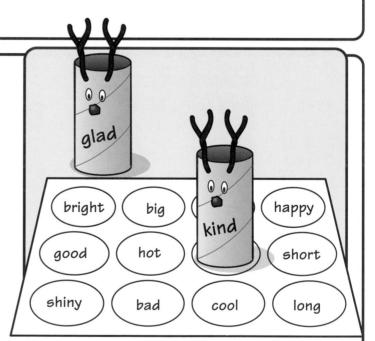

**Setting up the center:**
1. Assemble each reindeer as shown.
2. Choose 12 synonym word pairs. Program each reindeer with one word from each pair.
3. Draw twelve 2½-inch circles on the construction paper. Program each circle with a remaining word from each synonym pair.
4. Program the back of each reindeer with its matching synonym for self-checking.
5. Display the reindeer and construction paper at a center.

**Using the center:**
1. A student reads the word on each reindeer and places it on the corresponding circle.
2. After placing all of the reindeer, he checks his work by reading the back of each reindeer.

# Down the Chimney!

**Skill:** Matching rhyming words

**Materials needed:**
- five 9" x 12" sheets of red construction paper
- 5 empty Pringles® potato crisp cans
- glue
- five 1" x 8" strips of cotton batting
- permanent markers
- 15 construction paper Santa cutouts

**Setting up the center:**
1. Draw a brick pattern on each sheet of construction paper. Wrap each paper around a different can and glue the overlapping edges. Glue a strip of cotton batting around the top of each can.
2. Program each chimney with a rhyming word, such as *bat, night,* or *shop.*
3. For each chimney, program three Santa cutouts each with a different word that rhymes with the word on the chimney.
4. Write the appropriate rhyming words on the bottom of each can.

**Using the center:**
1. A student reads the word on each cutout. She places the Santa in the corresponding chimney.
2. After placing all of the Santas, she checks her work by reading the words on the bottom of each chimney.

# Guess the Gift

**Skill:** Critical thinking

**Materials needed:**
- discarded toy catalogs and toy store advertisements
- scissors
- glue
- a class supply of 8" newsprint squares
- markers
- a class supply of 8" construction paper squares
- a class supply of index cards
- a gift bag

**Setting up the center:**
1. Follow the directions below to make one gift. Then place the gift in the gift bag.
2. Display the gift bag and remaining materials at a center.

**Using the center:**
1. A student cuts out one picture of a toy and glues it on a square of newsprint.
2. He decorates a square of construction paper to resemble wrapping paper. He applies a thin line of glue to the top of the newsprint square and places the wrapping paper on it.
3. He writes three clues about his toy on an index card and glues the card on the gift to resemble a gift tag. He places his gift in the gift bag.
4. He chooses another gift from the bag, reads the clues on the tag, and attempts to guess the gift. He checks his guess by opening the gift.

# Don't Forget the Bows!

**Skill:** Creating and reading a graph

**Materials needed:**
- varying numbers of 2–3" red, green, blue, and yellow bows (fewer than 9 of each color)
- a large recycled gift bag
- a large paper grid (similar to the grid on page 169)
- a class supply of the "Don't Forget the Bows" form on page 169
- pencils
- crayons

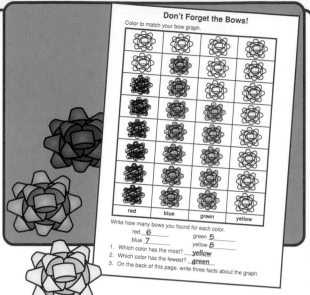

**Setting up the center:**
1. Store the bows in the gift bag and put it at a center. Place the grid on the floor nearby.
2. Display the forms, pencils, and crayons at the center.

**Using the center:**
1. A student removes the bows from the bag and sorts them by color.
2. She places each bow on the large paper grid.
3. She records her results on a form and follows the directions to complete it.

# Ornament Order

**Skill:** Ordering numbers

**Materials needed:**
- a permanent marker
- 12 plastic Christmas tree ornaments
- twelve 3" pipe cleaner lengths
- a decorated box
- masking tape
- one 5' length of garland

**Setting up the center:**
1. Program each ornament with a different two- or three-digit number.
2. Insert a pipe cleaner into the top opening of each ornament and secure it to the ornament by twisting. Bend the other end of to form a hook.
3. On the bottom of the decorated box, write the ornament numbers from least to greatest. Store the ornaments in the box.
4. Use tape to suspend the garland between two adjacent walls. Display the box nearby.

**Using the center:**
1. A student selects a predetermined number of ornaments from the box and hangs them on the garland.
2. He notes the numbers on each ornament and then puts them in order of sequence.
3. He continues in this manner until all the ornaments are hanging on the garland. He then turns over the box and checks his work.

# It's Kwanzaa Time!

**Skill:** Researching facts

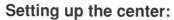

**Materials needed:**
- a variety of art supplies
- a photo album with 2 slip-in photo slots for each student
- 2 lined index cards for each student
- an assortment of Kwanzaa books
- pencils
- markers

**Setting up the center:**
1. Use the art supplies to decorate the photo album cover to reflect the Kwanzaa holiday.
2. Display the album, index cards, books, pencils, and markers at a center.

**Using the center:**
1. A student looks through the books and then chooses a fact about Kwanzaa that interests her.
2. She writes the fact in her own words on the lined side of an index card. On the blank side of another index card, she illustrates the fact.
3. She slides each card into the next available album slot.

# Kwanzaa Fruit Basket

**Skill:** Adding numbers

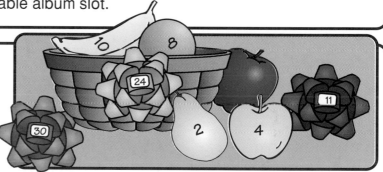

**Materials needed:**
- a permanent marker
- a calculator
- 10 pieces of assorted plastic fruits
- a basket with the hook side of a piece of self-adhesive Velcro® attached to the front center
- 10 white self-adhesive labels
- 10 bows (red, green, and black), each with the loop side of a piece of self-adhesive Velcro attached to the back

**Setting up the center:**
1. Program each piece of fruit with a different number from 1 to 10. Store the fruit in the basket.
2. For each bow, write a different sum on a label to correspond with the addends on one or more combinations of fruit. Then attach each label to the top of a different bow.
3. Display the basket, bows, and calculator at a center.

**Using the center:**
1. A student removes the fruit from the basket and arranges it on a table or workspace.
2. He attaches a bow to the basket and then places pieces of fruit inside it that add up to the sum on the bow. He uses the calculator to check his work.
3. He removes the bow and fruit from the basket and repeats the activity until all the bows have been used.

## New Year Rhymes

**Skill:** Sorting rhyming words

**Materials needed:**
- a permanent marker
- 15 cone-shaped party hats
- 5 different-colored markers
- pencils
- a class supply of lined paper

**Setting up the center:**
1. Use the marker to program a set of three hats with different rhyming words. Repeat this four times to create different sets of rhyming words with the remaining sets of hats.
2. For self-checking, use a marker to program the inside of each hat in a set. Program the remaining four sets with the remaining markers.
3. Display the hats, pencils, and paper at a center.

**Using the center:**
1. A student reads the word on each hat. She sorts the hats by their rhyming words.
2. To check her work, she turns over each set of hats to make sure the colors match.
3. On a sheet of paper, she writes a predetermined number of additional rhyming words for each set of words.

## New Year's Numbers

**Skill:** Understanding place value

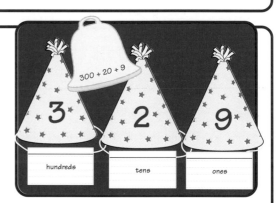

**Materials needed:**
- a permanent marker
- 10 cone-shaped party hats
- a supply of seasonal cutouts
- a resealable plastic bag
- 4 index cards
- transparent tape

**Setting up the center:**
1. Program each hat with a different number from 0 to 9.
2. Write the expanded notation of a different number on each cutout, making sure each number has no repeating digits. Program the back of each cutout with the correct answer for self-checking. Store the cutouts in the plastic bag.
3. Make "thousands," "hundreds," "tens," and "ones" index card labels. Then tape them to a center table in the correct order as a place value guide for students.
4. Display the bag and hats at the center.

**Using the center:**
1. A student removes the cutouts from the bag and arranges them with the expanded notations faceup on the table.
2. He reads the cutout and then places the corresponding numbered hats behind the place value labels to show his answer. He turns over the cutout to check his work. He repeats the activity until he has completed all the expanded notations.

# Martin Luther King Acrostics

**Skill:** Writing acrostics

**Materials needed:**
- markers
- at least 4 sheets of chart paper
- a supply of 1" paper squares
- 2 plastic jars
- a dictionary

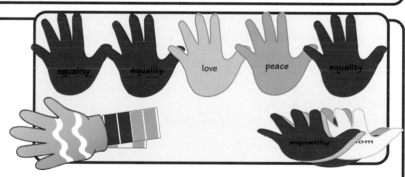

**F**airness
**R**espect
**E**qual
**E**nd fighting
**D**on't forget Martin Luther King Jr.
**O**ther people's feelings are important.
**M**anners

**D**are to dream.
**R**
**E**xcellent speaker
**A**
**M**

**Setting up the center:**
1. Write a different word—such as *freedom, dream, peace,* or *truth*—vertically on each sheet of chart paper. Make sure there is at least one letter for each student in your class.
2. Program each paper square with a letter to match one of the chart letters.
3. Label one jar "Pick a letter" and store the letter squares in it. Label the other jar "Discard."
4. Display the jars, chart paper, markers, and dictionary at a center.

**Using the center:**
1. A student reads each chart paper word and then removes a letter square from the "Pick a letter" jar.
2. Using a matching chart paper letter as the first letter in a word or phrase, she writes a word or phrase relating to Martin Luther King Jr. She refers to the dictionary whenever necessary.
3. She deposits the letter square in the "Discard" jar so that it is not used by another student.

# Hands Up for Peace

**Skill:** Extending patterns

**Materials needed:**
- blue, red, yellow, and green crayons
- 10 index cards
- a marker
- 40 or more student-cut construction paper hand cutouts (at least 10 of each crayon color)
- a glove

**Setting up the center:**
1. Use the crayons to make a different pattern of colors on each index card. Insert the cards into the glove.
2. Write a different word—such as *peace, love, equality,* or *freedom*—on each set of hand cut-outs.
3. Display the glove and hand cutouts at a center.

**Using the center:**
1. A student removes the pattern cards from the glove and then stacks them faceup on a table. He then sorts the hand cutouts by color.
2. He extends the top card's pattern by arranging corresponding hand cutouts and repeating the pattern. He then sets the pattern card aside and sorts the cutouts again.
3. The student continues in this manner until each pattern card has been used.

# Chinese New Year Chart

**Skills:** Reading a chart, building vocabulary

**Materials needed:**
- 1 copy of the chart at the top of page 170
- a class supply of 12" x 18" white construction paper
- fine-tipped markers
- a dictionary

**Setting up the center:**
Display the materials at a center.

**Using the center:**
1. A student locates her birth year on the chart. She then writes the corresponding animal name and her birth year at the top of a sheet of construction paper.
2. She draws a picture of the animal in the middle of her paper and then uses the chart to find her animal's characteristics. She writes the characteristics around her animal drawing.
3. At the bottom of her paper, the student writes her own definition for each characteristic and checks her work using the dictionary.

Use with "Chinese New Year Chart" on page 152.

### The Chinese Fortune Calendar
Each year is represented by 1 of 12 animals.

| Animal | Years | Characteristics |
|---|---|---|
| rat | 1984, 1996, 2008 | charming, hardworking, thrifty, clever |
| ox | 1985, 1997, 2009 | patient, dependable, fair-minded, alert |
| tiger | 1986, 1998, 2010 | competitive, unpredictable, a leader, daring |
| hare | 1987, 1999, 2011 | gracious, humble, quiet, kind |
| dragon | 1988, 2000, 2012 | strong, energetic, a leader, soft-hearted |
| snake | 1989, 2001, 2013 | wise, determined, secretive, graceful |
| horse | 1990, 2002, 2014 | energetic, impatient, confident, talkative |
| sheep | 1991, 2003, 2015 | artistic, caring, gentle, creative |
| monkey | 1992, 2004, 2016 | inventive, curious, smart, clever |
| rooster | 1993, 2005, 2017 | organized, alert, determined, self-centered |
| dog | 1994, 2006, 2018 | loyal, intelligent, affectionate, honest |
| boar | 1995, 2007, 2019 | tolerant, studious, quiet, good-hearted |

©2001 The Education Center, Inc. • Sensational Centers • TEC2859

**Rooster 1993**
determined self-centered
organized alert

1. *Organized* can mean neat. I am organized when I keep my desk clean.
2. *Determined* is when you want something and you don't give up.
3. *Alert* means you're awake and not sleepy.
4. *Self-centered* is when a person thinks of himself most of the time.

# Chinese New Year Animal Sort

**Skill:** Following written directions to classify items

**Materials needed:**
- an enlarged copy of the animal picture cards at the bottom of page 170
- scissors
- a supply of construction paper animal cutouts
- a marker
- a resealable plastic bag

Sort the animals into three groups by size.

**Setting up the center:**
1. Cut apart the animal picture cards.
2. On each animal cutout, write a different set of directions for sorting the animal picture cards.
3. Program the back of each cutout with the correct answers.
4. Store the animal picture cards and cutouts in the plastic bag and display the bag at a center.

**Using the center:**
1. A student removes an animal cutout and the animal picture cards from the bag and arranges them faceup on a table or workspace.
2. He choses a cutout and sorts the animal picture cards according to the directions. He then turns over the cutout to check his work.
3. He continues in this manner until he has followed the directions on each animal cutout.

# BROKEN HEARTS

**Skill:** Identifying and using contractions

**Materials needed:**
- 20 construction paper hearts
- markers
- scissors
- a 9" x 12" decorated envelope
- a class supply of lined paper
- pencils

**Setting up the center:**
1. Write a different contraction in the center of each of ten hearts. Program the back of each heart with the two words that make up the contraction.
2. For each contraction, program another heart with the two words that form that contraction. Cut the two-word hearts in half between the words. Store the hearts and heart halves in the envelope.
3. Display the envelope, paper, pencils, and markers at a center.

**Using the center:**
1. A student removes the hearts and heart halves from the bag and arranges them on a table or workspace. (Contractions should be faceup on whole hearts.)
2. She selects a heart and reads the contraction. She finds the matching heart halves and places them below the heart. She then turns over the whole heart to check her work. She continues in this manner until she has matched all heart halves to a heart.

# Heartfelt Conversations

**Skill:** Using quotations in a story

**Materials needed:**
- 5 large candy conversation hearts (select ones that are most appropriate)
- a snack-size resealable plastic bag
- a bowl of candy conversation hearts for munching
- a supply of lined paper
- pencils
- markers or crayons

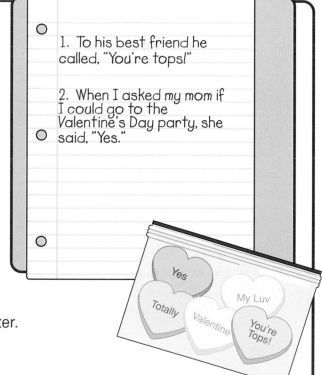

**Setting up the center:**
1. Seal the five large candy hearts in the bag.
2. Display the bag, bowl, paper, and pencils at a center.

**Using the center:**
1. A student reads the word or phrase on a heart through the bag.
2. He writes a sentence, putting that word or phrase in quotation marks.
3. He continues in this manner until he has written five sentences, each time using a different candy heart word or phrase.
4. If time allows, he illustrates each sentence on the back of his paper.

153

# Valentine's Mystery Bags

**Skills:** Describing, deductive reasoning

**Materials needed:**
- a supply of paper lunch bags, decorated as described
- a variety of valentine-related objects

**Setting up the center:**
1. Place one object in each paper bag.
2. Display the bags at a center.

**Using the center:**
1. One student from a pair chooses a bag and looks inside at the enclosed object.
2. She gives her partner a descriptive one-word clue about the object.
3. The partner tries to name the object.
4. If an incorrect guess is made, another clue is given. Guessing continues until the object is correctly identified.
5. After a correct guess, the students switch roles and a new bag is selected.
6. If time allows, partners may play another round.

# Heartfelt Stories

**Skill:** Creative writing

One day my sweetheart left me a note in my mailbox. It said, "I love you. Be mine." I said, "Yes!"

**Materials needed:**
- a class supply of 9" x 12" pink construction paper
- 2 bags of conversation hearts
- scissors
- a bowl
- a tablespoon
- a supply of napkins
- pencils
- crayons or markers

**Setting up the center:**
1. Cut each sheet of construction paper into a large heart shape.
2. Put the conversation hearts in the bowl.
3. Display the heart cutouts, bowl of candy, spoon, napkins, pencils, and crayons or markers at a center.

**Using the center:**
1. A student scoops a spoonful of conversation hearts onto his napkin.
2. He reads the words on each heart.
3. He writes a story on his cutout that includes the words from each candy heart.
4. He uses crayons or markers to decorate his heart cutout, and then he eats his candy.
5. He places his story in a designated display area.

# Cupid's Clothesline

**Skill:** Identifying place value

**Materials needed:**

- 10 construction paper copies of the cupid and heart patterns on page 171
- a marker
- a length of string or clothesline
- a supply of spring-type clothespins
- a marker

*Make a three digit number with:*
*6 in the tens place*
*3 in the hundreds place*
*2 in the ones place*

**Setting up the center:**

1. Program each heart with a number from 0 to 9.
2. On each cupid, write directions for making a multidigit number as shown. Label the back of each cupid with the number for self-checking.
3. Hang the clothesline in an area above a center. Display the cutouts and clothespins at the center.

**Using the center:**

1. A student selects a cupid cutout and reads the directions for making a number.
2. She uses clothespins to clip the numbered hearts to the clothesline in the correct order.
3. After clipping the hearts, she checks her work by looking at the back of the cupid cutout.
4. If time allows, she may select another cupid cutout and make a different number.

# Subtracting Sweets

**Skill:** Practicing subtraction

**Materials needed:**

- an empty heart-shaped candy box, candy liners included
- craft glue
- a supply of sticky dots
- a marker
- a supply of 1½" pom-poms
- a resealable plastic bag

**Setting up the center:**

1. Glue each candy liner to the bottom of the box.
2. Write a subtraction equation on a sticky dot and its corresponding answer on a different dot. Repeat this for each candy liner.
3. Place each answer sticker in the center of a liner. Program the inside of the box lid with matching equations and answers.
4. Glue each subtraction-problem sticker to a pom-pom. Allow the glue to dry. Store the pom-poms in the resealable bag.
5. Display the box and bag at a center.

**Using the center:**

1. A student selects a pom-pom and reads the subtraction problem.
2. He places the pom-pom in the wrapper programmed with the correct answer. To check his work, he turns over the box lid.

# Clever Clovers

**Skill:** Identifying fact families

**Materials needed:**
- a class set of the "Be a Clever Clover!" form on page 172
- 2 dice
- pencils

**Setting up the center:**
Display the materials at a center.

**Using the center:**
1. A student rolls the dice.
2. She writes the number showing on each die in the boxes on the clover stem.
3. She writes the sum of the two numbers in the circle.
4. She writes one fact on each leaflet to complete a fact family.
5. She repeats Steps 1–4 three more times to complete her paper.

# Pot of Gold

**Skills:** Counting and adding money

**Materials needed:**
- a supply of bingo chips spray-painted gold
- a permanent marker
- a small pot
- a supply of lined paper
- pencils
- a calculator

**Setting up the center:**
1. Program each painted chip with a coin amount: "1¢," "5¢," "10¢," or "25¢."
2. Place the chips in the pot.
3. Display the pot, paper, and pencils at a center.

**Using the center:**
1. A student scoops two small handfuls of coins from the pot. He adds the value of the coins in each handful and records the two amounts on his paper.
2. He adds the two amounts together and records that answer on his paper. He uses the calculator to check his work.
3. He returns the coins to the pot and continues in the same manner a predetermined number of times.

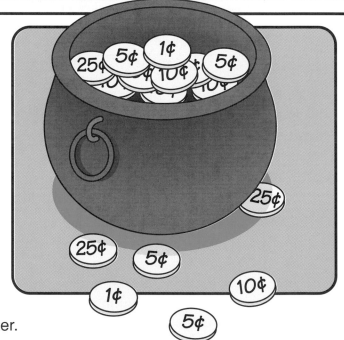

# Flower Power

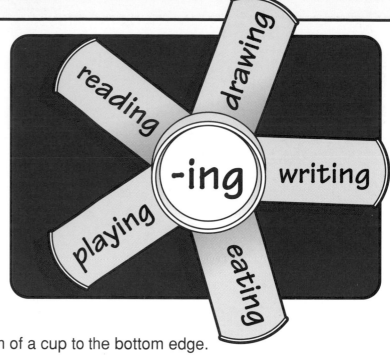

**Skill:** Using suffixes

**Materials needed:**
- a class supply of paper cups
- scissors
- a list of suffixes
- permanent markers
- a dictionary

**Setting up the center:**
Display the materials at a center.

**Using the center:**
1. A student makes five cuts from the rim of a cup to the bottom edge.
2. She folds down each resulting strip.
3. She turns the cup over (bottom side facing up) to display the resulting flower.
4. She chooses a suffix and writes it on the flower center.
5. She uses a dictionary to find five words ending in that suffix. She writes each word on a different petal.
6. She places the flower in a designated display area.

# A Critter Story

**Skill:** Creative writing

**Materials needed:**
- pencils
- a supply of construction paper scraps of various colors
- scissors
- a class supply of 1" x 3" construction paper strips
- glue
- a class supply of blank paper
- crayons or markers

**Setting up the center:**
Display the materials at a center.

**Using the center:**
1. A student draws and then cuts out a bug from a scrap of construction paper.
2. He draws facial features and legs on the bug.
3. He accordion-folds a paper strip and glues one end to the top of a blank sheet of paper. He glues the back of his bug to the other end of the strip.
4. He writes a springtime story about his bug's adventures and then adds illustrations to his paper using crayons or markers.

# Spring Garden

**Skill:** Sorting even and odd numbers

**Materials needed:**
- a green egg carton
- scissors
- a permanent marker
- 12 construction paper flowers, each glued to a different craft stick

**Setting up the center:**
1. Turn the egg carton upside down. Use scissors to make a small slit in each cup bottom.
2. Label the cups in one row "even" and the cups in the other row "odd" as shown.
3. Program the centers of six flowers with different even numbers and the centers of the other six flowers with different odd numbers.
4. For self-checking, write "e" or "o" on the back of each flower.
5. Display the carton and the flowers at a center.

**Using the center:**
1. A student selects a flower and determines if the number on it is even or odd.
2. She inserts the flower in the correct row of the carton.
3. After placing all the flowers, she checks her work by looking at the back of each flower.

# Seasonal Symmetry

**Skill:** Creating symmetrical drawings

**Materials needed:**
- a supply of spring-related greeting cards
- scissors
- a class supply of drawing paper
- glue
- pencils
- markers or crayons

**Setting up the center:**
1. Cut the front off each card. Discard the backs of the cards.
2. Cut each card front in half.
3. Display the card halves, paper, glue, pencils, and markers or crayons at a center.

**Using the center:**
1. A student chooses a card half and glues it to a sheet of paper.
2. He draws a symmetrical image to mirror the card half.
3. To complete the activity, he colors the drawing to match the card half.
4. He places the completed drawing in a designated display area.

# Cracked Eggs

**Skill:** Identifying long and short vowels

**Materials needed:**
- 10 egg-shaped tagboard cutouts in a variety of colors
- markers
- scissors
- a basket

**Setting up the center:**
1. Program each egg with a word on one end and its vowel sound on the other end.
2. Use a different zigzag cut to halve each egg and then place the halves in a basket.
3. Display the basket at a center.

**Using the center:**
1. A student removes the cutouts from the basket and arranges them on a table or workspace.
2. She selects a word and matches it to the correct vowel sound, making a complete egg.
3. After pairing all the egg halves, she checks her work by noting whether the zigzag cuts fit together properly.

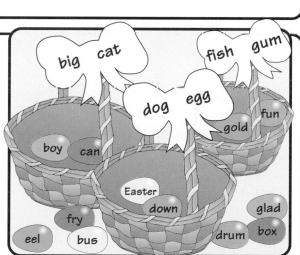

# Guide Me Down the Bunny Trail

**Skill:** Using guide words

**Materials needed:**
- 3 construction paper bow cutouts
- a permanent marker
- a dictionary
- tape
- 3 baskets
- 15 plastic eggs

**Setting up the center:**
1. Label each bow cutout with two guide words from a page in the dictionary. Tape one bow to each basket.
2. Program each set of five eggs with words that come alphabetically between the guide words on each bow.
3. Display the baskets, eggs, and dictionary at a center.

**Using the center:**
1. A student selects an egg and reads the word written on it.
2. He decides which guide words come alphabetically before and after the word on the egg. He then places the egg in the correct basket.
3. He continues in the same manner until he has placed all of the eggs.
4. He checks his work by finding each word on the correct dictionary page.

# Easter Addition

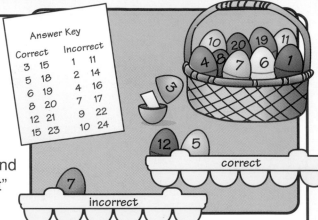

**Skill:** Solving addition problems

**Materials needed:**
- 24 construction paper strips
- a permanent marker
- 24 plastic eggs
- a sheet of paper
- a basket
- 2 egg cartons, one labeled "Correct" and the other "Incorrect"

**Setting up the center:**
1. Program each of ten construction paper strips with a correctly solved addition problem. Program each remaining strip with an incorrectly solved addition problem.
2. Label each strip and plastic egg with numbers 1–24. Create an answer key, like the one shown, indicating the problem numbers that are correct and incorrect. Place each strip in its corresponding plastic egg.
3. Place the eggs and folded answer key in the basket.
4. Display the basket and egg cartons at a center.

**Using the center:**
1. A student draws an egg from the basket. She opens the egg, reads the problem, and decides whether it is solved correctly or incorrectly.
2. She returns the problem to the egg and then places the egg in the appropriate carton.
3. After placing the eggs, she checks her work using the answer key.

# Easter Riddles

**Skill:** Solving problems

**Materials needed:**
- 10 index cards
- a permanent marker
- 10 plastic eggs
- a basket

*I am a two-digit number. The sum of my digits is 5. I am an odd number. What number am I?*

C

**Setting up the center:**
1. Program each index card with a riddle like the one shown.
2. Label each card and the inside of a corresponding egg with a letter for self-checking. Program the outside of each egg with the answer to the riddle.
3. Place the eggs and index cards in a basket. Display the basket at a center.

**Using the center:**
1. The student chooses a card and reads the riddle.
2. He selects the egg from the basket that shows the answer to the riddle.
3. To check his work, he opens the egg and compares the letter shown with the letter on the card.
4. The student continues in the same manner for a predetermined number of problems.

# Feed the Bunny

**Skill:** Identifying nouns and verbs

**Materials needed:**
- scissors
- markers or crayons
- two 9" x 12" sheets of orange construction paper
- a copy of the bunny pattern on page 173
- a manila envelope

**Setting up the center:**
1. Cut out 20 construction paper carrots. Program each carrot with a noun or a verb.
2. Color and cut out the bunny pattern. Laminate the bunny and carrots for durability, if desired.
3. Program the back of the envelope with an answer key, showing which words are nouns and which are verbs.
4. Place the carrots in the envelope. Display the bunny and envelope at a center.

**Using the center:**
1. A student chooses a carrot and decides if the word shown is a noun or a verb.
2. She places the carrot on the appropriately labeled paw.
3. After placing all the carrots, she checks her work using the answer key.

# Jelly Bean Bonanza

**Skills:** Solving addition facts, reading a chart

Jelly Bean Chart
red = 1
yellow = 2
orange = 3
green = 4
purple = 5
white = 6
black = 7

**Materials needed:**
- 10 resealable plastic bags, numbered 1–10
- a supply of jelly beans
- a permanent marker
- construction paper egg cutout
- a class supply of lined paper
- pencils

**Setting up the center:**
1. Place six jelly beans in each bag.
2. Determine a value for each jelly bean, such as "red = 1." Program the front of the egg-shaped cutout with a chart listing the value of each color of jelly bean. Program the back of the cutout with the total value of the jelly beans in each bag.
3. Place the bags, egg cutout, paper, and pencils at a center.

**Using the center:**
1. The student selects a bag and removes the jelly beans. He uses the chart to determine the value of each jelly bean.
2. The student totals the value of the jelly beans and writes the amount on his paper.
3. He checks his work by turning over the egg cutout.
4. The student returns the jelly beans to the bag. If time allows, he continues in the same manner a predetermined number of times.

# CINCO SEARCH

**Skill:** Researching

**Materials needed:**
- a supply of self-adhesive labels
- a class supply of cutouts of the postcard pattern on page 174
- books related to Cinco de Mayo
- pencils
- markers or crayons

**Setting up the center:**
1. Program each label with a vocabulary word important to Cinco de Mayo, such as "fireworks."
2. Display the labels, postcard cutouts, books, pencils, and markers or crayons at a center.

**Using the center:**
1. A student chooses a label and places it in a corner on the blank side of the postcard (see illustration).
2. She researches how the vocabulary word is related to the holiday of Cinco de Mayo.
3. On the front left-hand side of the postcard, the student writes a note to a friend or relative, briefly describing how the holiday is celebrated and how her selected word is related to it.
4. She addresses the postcard on the right, draws a stamp in the appropriate space, and illustrates her writing on the back.

# Candy Confusion

**Skill:** Solving problems

**Materials needed:**
- a manila envelope
- a copy of the piñata and candy patterns on page 175
- markers or crayons
- scissors
- a pencil
- glue

**Setting up the center:**
1. Program the top half of the envelope with the clues listed on the pattern page.
2. Color the piñata pattern and candies as shown.
3. Cut out the piñata pattern and glue it to the bottom half of the envelope.
4. Cut out the candies. Use a pencil to number the back of each candy, as shown, for self-checking. Laminate the candies, if desired. Place the candies in the envelope.
5. Display the envelope at a center.

**Using the center:**
1. The student removes the candies from the envelope. He reads the clues and then arranges the candies in the correct order.
2. After placing all of the candies, he checks his work by looking on the back of the candies.

# Summer Scene

**Skill:** Following directions

**Materials needed:**
- transparent tape
- a sheet of poster board, decorated with a tree as shown
- ten 4" leaf cutouts, numbered 1–10
- markers or crayons
- a class supply of drawing paper

**Setting up the center:**
1. Tape the leaves to the tree so that each leaf can be lifted.
2. Program the area hidden by each leaf with a direction for drawing a summer picture. (See example shown.)
3. Display the poster, markers or crayons, and paper at a center.

**Using the center:**
1. A student takes a sheet of drawing paper.
2. Beginning with leaf number 1, she lifts each leaf on the poster board in order and follows the directions to create a picture.
3. If time allows, she may create a different summer picture using the same directions.

# Summer Word Scramble

**Skill:** Building words

**Materials needed:**
- a numbered list of words related to summer
- a supply of seashells or ceramic tiles
- a permanent marker
- a supply of resealable plastic bags
- a plastic sand pail
- a class supply of lined paper
- pencils

**Setting up the center:**
1. Program each letter of the first word on a different seashell or tile. Store the shells or tiles in a resealable plastic bag labeled with the number 1. Repeat for each remaining word on the list.
2. Place the bags and folded word list in a pail.
3. Display the pail, paper, and pencils at a center.

**Using the center:**
1. A student takes a bag from the pail and removes the shells or tiles. He arranges them to spell a word.
2. He writes the number from the bag and the word on a sheet of paper. He returns the shells or tiles to the bag.
3. The student continues in the same manner for a predetermined number of words.
4. To check his work, he refers to the word list.

# Summer Scoops

**Skill:** Identifying fact and opinion

**Materials needed:**
- 20 cutouts of the ice-cream-scoop pattern on page 83
- a permanent marker
- 2 disposable bowls, labeled "Fact" and "Opinion"

**Setting up the center:**
1. Program each ice-cream-scoop cutout with a fact or an opinion about any topic.
2. Label the back of each cutout "F" or "O" for self-checking.
3. Laminate the cutouts for durability, if desired.
4. Display the cutouts and bowls at a center.

**Using the center:**
1. The student chooses an ice-cream scoop. She reads the sentence shown and decides if it is a fact or an opinion.
2. She places the scoop in the correct bowl.
3. After placing the scoops, she refers to the back of each cutout to check her work.

# Summer Time

**Skill:** Telling time

**Materials needed:**
- 10 cutouts of the clock pattern on page 176
- 10 yellow construction paper cutouts of the sun pattern on page 176
- a marker

**Setting up the center:**
1. Program hands on each clock pattern for the desired skill level.
2. Write a matching digital time on each sun pattern.
3. Label the back of each matching pair with a number or letter for self-checking.
4. Display the cutouts at a center.

**Using the center:**
1. The student selects a clock pattern. He reads the time shown.
2. He places the clock over the sun pattern that shows the matching digital time.
3. After placing all the clocks, the student turns over each cutout to check his work.

# Savvy Thanksgiving Consumers

Read your advertisement.
Use the ad to answer the questions below.

1. What is the name of the product? _____

2. What is the brand name? _____

3. What store is advertising the product? _____

4. How much does the product cost? _____

5. What other information does the ad tell you? _____

6. Is there something you would like to know that the ad does not tell you?

   _____

   _____

7. What would you do differently if you were advertising this product? _____

   _____

8. Draw a picture of what your ad would look like.

# Snowman Decorations

Put a check mark next to each answer that describes you.
Then follow the directions to make decorations for your snowman.

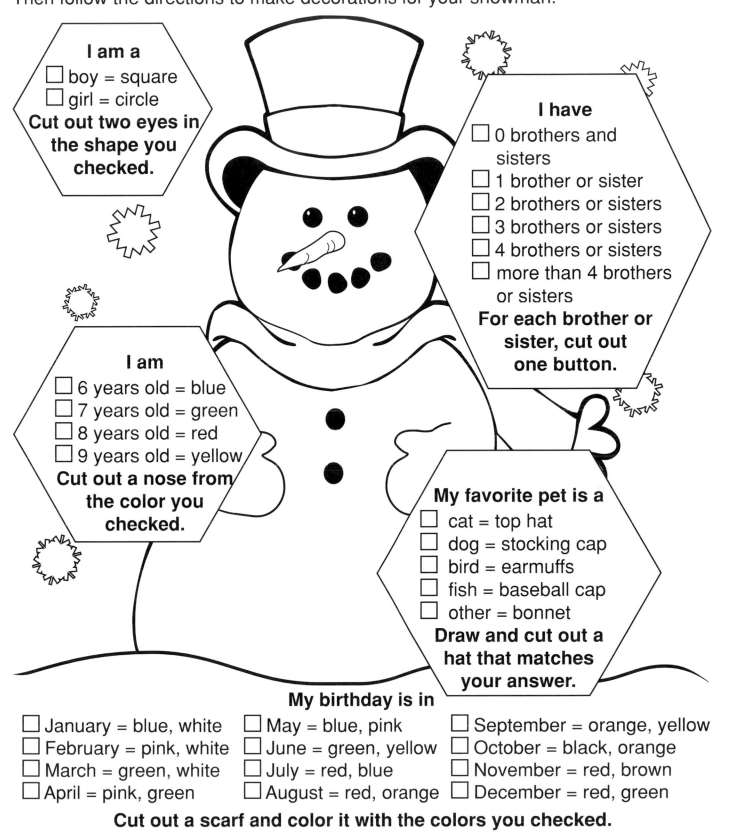

**I am a**
- ☐ boy = square
- ☐ girl = circle

**Cut out two eyes in the shape you checked.**

**I have**
- ☐ 0 brothers and sisters
- ☐ 1 brother or sister
- ☐ 2 brothers or sisters
- ☐ 3 brothers or sisters
- ☐ 4 brothers or sisters
- ☐ more than 4 brothers or sisters

**For each brother or sister, cut out one button.**

**I am**
- ☐ 6 years old = blue
- ☐ 7 years old = green
- ☐ 8 years old = red
- ☐ 9 years old = yellow

**Cut out a nose from the color you checked.**

**My favorite pet is a**
- ☐ cat = top hat
- ☐ dog = stocking cap
- ☐ bird = earmuffs
- ☐ fish = baseball cap
- ☐ other = bonnet

**Draw and cut out a hat that matches your answer.**

**My birthday is in**

| | | |
|---|---|---|
| ☐ January = blue, white | ☐ May = blue, pink | ☐ September = orange, yellow |
| ☐ February = pink, white | ☐ June = green, yellow | ☐ October = black, orange |
| ☐ March = green, white | ☐ July = red, blue | ☐ November = red, brown |
| ☐ April = pink, green | ☐ August = red, orange | ☐ December = red, green |

**Cut out a scarf and color it with the colors you checked.**

**Note to the teacher:** Use with "Snowman Glyphs" on page 143.

# Spin the Dreidel

A top called a *dreidel* is used to play a favorite Hanukkah game. The letters on the sides of a dreidel are the first letters of four Hebrew words meaning "A great miracle happened there."

**Directions:** Spin the dreidel and make a tally mark next to the picture of the side of the dreidel that is showing. Spin the dreidel a total of 20 times and then write the total number of spins next to each set of tally marks. Then answer the questions at the bottom of the page.

| | Tally | Total |
|---|---|---|
| shin | _____ | _____ |
| hay | _____ | _____ |
| gimel | _____ | _____ |
| nun | _____ | _____ |

Which symbol has the highest total number of spins?_____

Which symbol has the lowest total number of spins?_____

# Don't Forget the Bows!

Color to match your bow graph.

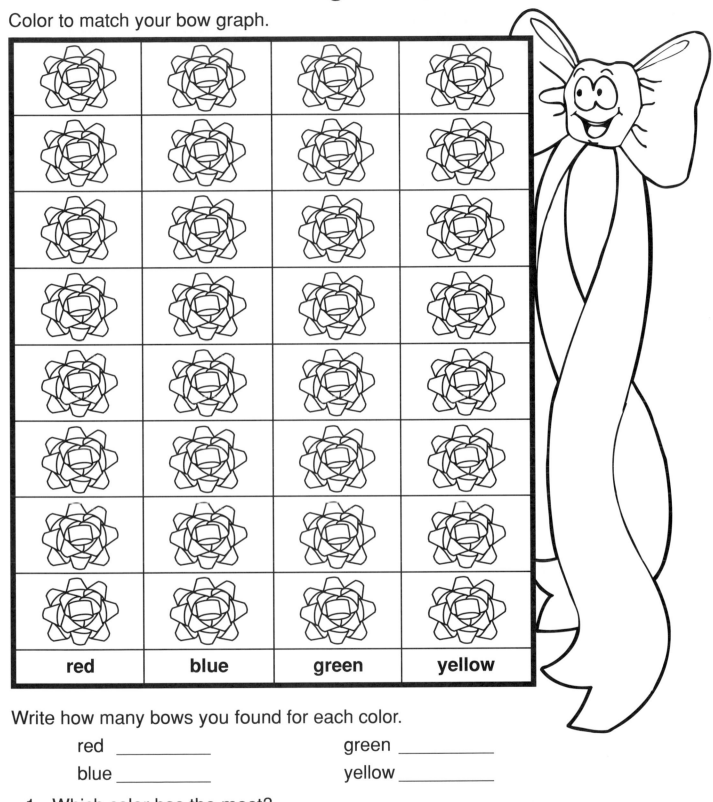

| red | blue | green | yellow |

Write how many bows you found for each color.

red _____     green _____

blue _____     yellow _____

1. Which color has the most? _____

2. Which color has the fewest? _____

3. On the back of this page, write three facts about the graph.

**Note to the teacher:** Use with "Don't Forget the Bows!" on page 148.

# Chinese Fortune Calendar
Use with "Chinese New Year Chart" on page 152.

| Animal | Years | Characteristics |
|---|---|---|
| rat | 1984, 1996, 2008 | charming, hardworking, thrifty, clever |
| ox | 1985, 1997, 2009 | patient, dependable, fair-minded, alert |
| tiger | 1986, 1998, 2010 | competitive, unpredictable, a leader, daring |
| hare | 1987, 1999, 2011 | gracious, humble, quiet, kind |
| dragon | 1988, 2000, 2012 | strong, energetic, a leader, soft-hearted |
| snake | 1989, 2001, 2013 | wise, determined, secretive, graceful |
| horse | 1990, 2002, 2014 | energetic, impatient, confident, talkative |
| sheep | 1991, 2003, 2015 | artistic, caring, gentle, creative |
| monkey | 1992, 2004, 2016 | inventive, curious, smart, clever |
| rooster | 1993, 2005, 2017 | organized, alert, determined, self-centered |
| dog | 1994, 2006, 2018 | loyal, intelligent, affectionate, honest |
| boar | 1995, 2007, 2019 | tolerant, studious, quiet, good-hearted |

# Animal Picture Cards
Use with "Chinese New Year Animal Sort" on page 152.

Name _____

# Be a Clever Clover!

Follow the directions your teacher gives you to complete the fact-family clovers below.

A.

B.

C.

D.

**Note to the teacher:** Use with "Clever Clovers" on page 156.

noun

verb

# Postcard Patterns
Use with "Cinco Search" on page 162.

174     ©2001 The Education Center, Inc. • *Sensational Centers* • TEC2869

## Piñata and Candy Patterns

Use with "Candy Confusion" on page 162.

### Clues

1. The red and green candies are first and last.
2. The yellow candy is directly above the blue candy.
3. The orange candy is directly below the red candy.
4. There are two candies below the yellow candy.

# Clock and Sun Patterns
Use with "Summer Time" on page 164.